1981

CONTEMPORARY LATIN AMERICAN FICTION

CONTEMPORARY LATIN AMERICAN FICTION

CARPENTIER, SABATO, ONETTI, ROA,
DONOSO, FUENTES, GARCÍA MÁRQUEZ

Seven Essays

EDITED BY

SALVADOR BACARISSE

SCOTTISH ACADEMIC PRESS

EDINBURGH

1980

Reprinted from
FORUM FOR MODERN LANGUAGE STUDIES
Volume XV No. 2

Published by
Scottish Academic Press Ltd.
33 Montgomery Street, Edinburgh 7

SBN 7073 0255 2

This edition first published 1980

Printed in Great Britain by
W. C. Henderson & Son Ltd., St. Andrews

PREFACE

Our Western society often voices its pride in the benefits of commercial competition. No such admiration, however, is heard when a similar situation prevails in literature, when creative writers vie with each other for a share of a market avid to consume their imaginative products. Yet whatever its drawbacks, and there are some, the benefits are plain to see. Such was the situation in the sixties with the Latin American novelists. Older writers, like Borges and Asturias ("los does grandes renovadores" as Fuentes calls them), occupied their rightful place internationally. Those who had failed to make an impact at the start of their careers, such as Onetti and Lezama Lima, were revalued, and rightly so, in the wake of the success of Sabato, Carpentier, Rulfo, García Márquez, Cortázar, Fuentes and Vargas Llosa. Younger ones, like Donoso, Cabrera Infante, Sarduy, Puig and others, now had elders to emulate, while Roa Bastos *re*-entered the scene with his extraordinary *Yo el Supremo*. His novel is one of several, all published in the seventies, on the theme of power and the *caudillos*.

Whatever the publicity machinery of the publishing houses may have done to boost a favourable situation, the undeniable fact is that we have now, in the so-called "nueva novela" (not a very homogeneous type, and only a distant cousin rather than a direct descendant of the *nouveau roman*) a body of literature—as opposed to popular fiction—of extraordinary variety and quality, which has found favour both in the academic world and with the reading public the world over. Putting together a volume of essays like the present one (and others might follow) responds, therefore, to a double need: to assess on scholarly grounds some of the more representative works of these writers and to acquaint the reading public with some of the hidden riches of the literature already in their hands.

The seven essays collected here accurately reflect both the variety and the quality I have just mentioned. The writers studied fall broadly into two groups: those with a predominant concern with the world and its problems over and above aesthetic ones, and those holding the opposite view· Carpentier, Roa, García Márquez, Fuentes and Sabato come into the first category; Onetti and Donoso into the second. This division, which is only partially valid anyway, obscures what is perhaps the most important point about the "nueva novela": its formal originality. None of the novels discussed here adheres to traditional 19th-century patterns. However, the first five do have paraphrasable contents, while the other two have not.

Carpentier, "nuestro gran clásico moderno" (in the words of Fuentes once more), who coined the phrase "lo real maravilloso", uses fantasy in a very different way from Borges and his novels are almost allegorical. Because of this, one is reluctant to speak of commitment, even in the loosest sense of the term. Yet Dr Martin is right, I think, when he says that Carpentier still believes "that the world can be denoted and stories simply narrated". But there is much more to *Los pasos perdidos* than the phrase suggests, as Dr Macdonald demonstrates. By portraying a self-deceiving narrator, Carpentier hides his faith in a solution to modern alienation. "Los pasos perdidos" will not be recovered unless the reader is alert to the radical irony underlying the novel. Macdonald thus takes the first and most important step in resolving the contradiction between Carpentier's pro-revolutionary views (after all, he is Fidel Castro's Ambassador in Paris) and the failed hero of this and other novels.

Roa Bastos addresses himself to his contemporaries too, by means of a vast historical metaphor. The life of Paraguay's first ruler, José Gaspar de Francia, which he narrates with a great display of historical sources and artistic devices—but with programmatic intentions for the future, according to Dr Martin—acts as this metaphor. Martin opens up an interesting debate: the place of irrationalism in revolutionary literature, for this irrationalism seems to me to be implied in his conclusion that *Yo el Supremo* brilliantly fuses "literary revolution" with "revolutionary literature".

A minor character in the long-awaited novel by García Márquez, *El otoño del patriarca*, enables Professor Brotherston to bring into this volume an important dimension which would otherwise be missing: the Indian. Brotherston's knowledge in this field establishes interesting connections between Saturno Santos and other Indian figures but, more importantly, brings out the unsuspected relevance of the Indian voice in the interpretation of this novel.

Fuentes is represented by one of the most widely studied and read of his novels, *La muerte de Artemio Cruz*. Fuentes combines critical realism, in the best tradition, with radical innovation in form. Professor Shaw is able to show that the dislocation of chronology creates a new sequence which has a subtle effect on the whole, an effect greater than that brought about by the alternating use of first-, second- and third-person narrative and one that cannot be discarded once the episodes have been rearranged conventionally after the reading of the novel. Fuentes is shown to be as much of an artist and master of his craft as a critic of Mexican society.

Another aspect of today's society is vividly reflected in Sabato's novel: the revival of religious thinking, the "boom" of the occult (as Colin Wilson calls it). The fantastic elements in *Abaddón, el exterminador* are not, as they are in Borges, expressive devices, nor are they constitutive of reality, as they are in Carpentier, but are true manifestations of a transcendent world that Sabato has devoted his whole life to exploring. However, in spite of Sabato's eloquent defence of irrationality, causality—whether historical, psychological or transcendental—remains paramount in his work. This creates the tension that makes it such an exhilarating experience to read *Abaddón* or to "explain" it.

There is really no way in which the remaining two writers, Onetti and Donoso, could be said to reflect current social issues in their societies, at least not in an obvious way, although Marxist critics and others have done just that. What is most striking in both *La muerte y la niña* and *El obsceno pájaro de la noche* is their obscurity, subdued in the first, strident in the second. Professor Terry and Dr Bacarisse cope with this difficulty in very different ways. For Terry, Onetti's novel raises the fundamental question of the autonomy of fiction, its self-sufficiency. The purpose of fiction is not to depict life, but itself. Language becomes, as Benedetti calls it, "el gran protagonista". *La muerte y la niña cannot* make sense, since it is being written by the very characters who people it and who "talk" when they appear to "act", and do so without reference to any pre-established facts. Of course, others, through philosophical convictions and by means of fictions still dependent on reality, have arrived at a picture of the world as absurd and meaningless as that of Onetti: Existentialist fiction, possibly the begetter of "autonomous" fiction.

Because it is possible to account for the same phenomenon in such diametrically-opposed ways, Dr Bacarisse's "explanation" of *El obsceno pájaro de la noche* is no less satisfying than Professor Terry's of Onetti's work. Pamela Bacarisse prefers to account for the internal contradictions in terms of a "mental state", of a strategy of self-defence on the part of the narrator which consists of systematically destroying his identity in order not to lose it! But cases of people who commit suicide in order to escape death are, of course, well known.

SALVADOR BACARISSE

St. Andrews,
April, 1979

CONTRIBUTORS

IAN MACDONALD has taught modern Spanish and Latin American literature at Aberdeen University since 1965. He is the author of a book on Gabriel Miró (London, 1975).

PAMELA BACARISSE went to Aberdeen University in 1969, and teaches Portuguese as well as modern Spanish and Latin American literature there. She has published articles on Cernuda, Pessoa, Sá-Carneiro and Manuel Puig. At present, she is working on Donoso's latest novel, *Casa de campo*.

DONALD SHAW is Professor of Hispanic Studies at the University of Edinburgh. He has published books on Rómulo Gallegos and Borges as well as on Spanish writers of the 19th and 20th centuries. He has also edited a novel by Mallea and has written several articles on both fields.

GORDON BROTHERSTON is Professor at Essex University. He has written books on Latin American poetry and the emergence of the Latin American novel and has edited a collection of Modernist poetry, *Ariel*, *Ficciones* of Borges and short stories. His new book, *Image of the New World*, is due to be published by Thames & Hudson this year.

ARTHUR TERRY is Professor of Literature at Essex University. His publications range from mediaeval Catalan, with a book on Ausiàs March, to modern Spanish literature (Antonio Machado). He is interested in the baroque—he is presently writing a book on 17th-century Spanish poetry—and Juan Carlos Onetti.

GERALD MARTIN is Director of Latin American Studies at Portsmouth Polytechnic and is a frequent visitor to Latin America. He has published several essays on Miguel Ángel Asturias and is a member of the international committee engaged in the publication of his Complete Works. His critical edition of *Hombres de maíz* is due out this year.

SALVADOR BACARISSE was born in Madrid and has lived in France and Spain as well as this country. He has taught modern Spanish and Latin American literature at St. Andrews University since 1965 and is Joint General Editor of *Forum for Modern Language Studies*. He has written articles on Realism and Galdós and on Sánchez Ferlosio, but for some time now has been researching into Latin American literature, particularly that of the River Plate and Cuba.

CONTENTS

I

MAGICAL ECLECTICISM:
LOS PASOS PERDIDOS
AND JEAN-PAUL SARTRE

"Invirtiendo, para uso propio, un principio filosófico que nos era común, solía decir que quien actuaba de 'modo automático era *esencia* sin *existencia*'." The speaker is the unnamed narrator of Alejo Carpentier's *Los pasos perdidos*. He is reporting the words of X.T.H., the leader of a small artistic group in New York around 1950, whom he presents as something of a charlatan.[1] Every reader will have been struck by the reference to the crucial principle of existentialism, "existence precedes essence", even though it is somewhat vulgarised by confusion with the idea of automatic action. Other references in *Los pasos perdidos* make it clear that this is post-war French *cave* existentialism. But a good number of puzzling ambiguities arise as soon as the reader pursues the theme. While the narrator mocks X.T.H.'s existentialism, he nevertheless seems to take for granted ("nos era común") the principle "existence precedes essence". Yet such a categorical assertion of the narrator's attachment to existentialism is rare; usually it is attributed, again mockingly, to the narrator's mistress Mouche: "A menudo me exasperaba por su dogmático apego a ideas y actitudes conocidas en las cervecerías de Saint-Germain-des-Prés, cuya estéril discusión me hacía huir de su casa con el ánimo de no volver" (30). Perhaps the narrator sees himself as an adherent of a rigorous philosophical existentialism chagrined by its vulgar debasement in the cellars of Paris?

Such questions apart, this intellectual background serves first of all to place the narrator and his friends with apparent precision into their cultural background, into what Carpentier elsewhere calls "una suerte de ecología

intelectual a la que el hombre, comprometido con su tiempo, escapa difícil-
mente".[2] Born during the Great War, the narrator is uprooted from his
Cuban home in adolescence and settled in the United States, whence he
travels in the late thirties to discover his European roots. His mistress
Mouche "se había formado intelectualmente en el gran baratillo surrealista"
(29), so that the cultural journey both have followed is from surrealism to a
sort of existentialism, passing through the experience of European war.
Mouche's position is the more clearly, though ironically, described. Surrealist
elements in her ideas are the most commonly mentioned: chance, evasion,
the unknown, Rimbaud (35) are forerunners of the more specific references
such as that to André Breton's "necesidad . . . de disparar sobre el primer
transeúnte" (77). Such references are mixed with those to existentialism—
clearly Mouche's mind is a rag-bag of the ideas of the thirties and forties.
But at the same time Carpentier seems deliberately, through his narrator,
to blur the focus. The reader is often puzzled as to how exactly to place a
particular cultural reference; it is not just a matter of his not knowing
enough: he feels, as it were, actively frustrated. The linguistic sign for this
is the narrator's obsessive use of the word "cierto". Speaking of Mouche's
role as a sort of groupie, apparently to the French surrealists, the narrator
refers to "las ideas estéticas de ciertas capillas literarias" (130). This wilful
device is almost always associated with descriptions of the cultural background: "ciertos ambientes artísticos" (50), "prolongada frecuentación de
ciertos ambientes" (75), "ciertas ideas me cansaban" (77), "ciertos temas de
la 'modernidad' me resultaban intolerables" (78), "del humo abyecto de
ciertas chimeneas" (101), "cierta famosa novela moderna" (105), "cierta
tradición es contrariada" (162), "de ciertos abrazos sin objeto, de ciertos
contactos exasperados" (262). This linguistic tic always serves to indicate
features of modern culture that the narrator dislikes, indicating his own
discomfort and ambivalence. But it also becomes established as an element
in a code that the reader has to crack by supplying his own cultural knowledge—a do-it-yourself element in the shaping of the novel. This cultural
knowledge is not just drawn upon in the unconscious or semi-conscious way
that art always requires; instead the reader is forced to be aware of his own
code-cracking activities. And as in the kind of competition which has a
number of alternative solutions, so the reader on occasion cannot entirely
clarify the reference—is it surrealism, is it existentialism, or is it something
else?

Thus we are led into a world that appears to offer a precise situation
taken from the real world, but make the jarring discovery that pieces of
it are slightly displaced or defocused. The technique is characteristic in
Carpentier, where device after device points to the fictionality of the text.
In *Los pasos perdidos* it is not even surprising since the novel may be seen
in one sense as a meditation on the problems of writing about Latin America
in the face of the texts of the past. Carpentier seems to have abandoned a

non-fictional version of his travels in Venezuela—*La gran sabana*—in the face of these problems, resorting instead to a fiction, and in particular to a first-person narrative whose radical irony enabled him to deal more adequately with his own perplexities.[3] This fiction, *Los pasos perdidos*, flaunts its status as a text, as an artefact. As a first-person narrative it makes no pretence of plausibility of origin. It cannot be a diary, nor can it have been written after the events it describes were completed: in that sense it is internally self-contradictory. The displacements and blurrings in the presentation of the cultural world fulfil a similar function.

An exactly parallel problem arises if the reader tries to place the action of the novel too precisely in terms of the time of the real world, for again the novel's realism is not quite what it seems. Eduardo G. González has examined the dates given in the novel and revealed the careful construction involved.[4] Amidst the complex structure there stands out the "error" that most readers will notice: in sub-chapter X the day of the week suddenly jumps ahead by one day. The novel had begun on Sunday, 4 June, which falls in 1950. Now it offers us Tuesday, 12 June, which is correct for 1951. The narrator makes a mistake which has symbolic implications that González and González Echevarría have elucidated.[5] But there is yet another "error": two days later the narrator describes the day as Corpus Christi, making it fall, quite correctly, on a Thursday. The narrator may have made a mistake in his account by skipping from Sunday to Tuesday, but the mistake has now assimilated itself to the reality of the novel. Furthermore, in 1951 Corpus fell on 24 May, and in 1950 on 8 June. 1949 offers the only remotely possible date, 16 June, as opposed to the 14 June of the novel. The original "error", if it is the author's, is compounded and if it is the narrator's, quite impermeable to any logic, internally self-contradictory.

What, in this situation, is to be made of the narrator's repeated references to his cultural background? It is worth trying to sort out more clearly their role in the novel, but always bearing in mind the intricate and treacherous structure in which they are held, and Carpentier's apparent desire to capture what Breton called the "interior model". Unavoidably the question can only be tackled by selection, and Jean-Paul Sartre offers a useful point of focus through which to examine at least the existentialist area in the cultural background.

Several critics have pointed out that there is an important Sartrean element in *Los pasos perdidos*, and Roberto González Echevarría writes of it: "The ideological framework of earlier works (mainly Spenglerian) is set off against a different and conflicting conception of man and history: Sartrean existentialism." He notes that Carpentier at this period attacked the concept of committed literature à la Sartre, but also that "Sartrean concepts like 'authenticity' . . . surface in this novel."[6] If the field is broadened to include the whole existentialist "event" of the thirties and forties the list of coincidences becomes very long. Authenticity and alienation would be accompanied by da-sein and the absurd, by anguish, bad faith, self-disgust, and commitment, by Camus' Sisyphus and Sartre's notion of absence, by a powerful interest in temporality and will, by the notions of the journey, the encounter, the threat of death, by the meaning of past and future, by the temptation and threat of the in-itself, by possibles and projects. All of these characteristic themes of existentialism appear in more or less obvious form in *Los pasos perdidos*.

But it is not a question of hunting down a list of undifferentiated sources and influences, many of them rather superficial. What is required is an examination of how these themes work within the novel. And in order to do this it is necessary to make a rigorous preliminary distinction. Early criticism of *Los pasos perdidos* tended to make the error of identifying Carpentier and his hero, talking in a general way about Carpentier's views on Latin America, on the artist, on surrealism and so on. Carpentier's *Nota* at the end of the novel gives, at first glance, encouragement to such a view, as does the discursive character of parts of the novel. Some coincidences between the life of hero and author can also be taken in this sense. Yet we have seen that Carpentier gave up a directly autobiographical account of his travels and chose instead a fictional form. Even without this information, the technique of the novel itself enforces a reading that clearly separates author and narrator. We are faced with an orthodox unreliable narrator, with the inevitable ironic subversion of his account.

If we pick on Sartre as a focal point through which to view existentialist elements in *Los pasos perdidos* we have therefore to separate the Sartrean element in the narrator from that in the author. There are two further distinctions of less consequence. First we can distinguish Sartre-in-the-narrator from Sartre-in-the-characters. We learn not only about the existentialist elements in the narrator, but also in, for instance, Mouche, who, as presented by the narrator, is the chief exponent of existentialist ideas in the novel. Even though Sartre is never mentioned by name, a popularized version of his views is clearly present as one element in her set of ideas. The narrator mocks these ideas, yet in part uses them himself. Several critics have pointed out that the narrator is constantly guilty of the faults he finds in Mouche, so that this presentation of existentialism in what at first seems a paradoxical way is in one sense simply a part of the narrator's self-deceiving character, and of his function as an unreliable narrator. The reader is always and simultaneously confronted with a double dislocation: his view is through the narrator's eyes and through the author's wilful shifts in internal and external reality.

Secondly, the author's use of Sartrean ideas must be distinguished from the possible use of them by the critic to analyse the novel as a whole. Existential psychoanalysis, for instance, could be a fruitful approach to the meaning of the narrator—what is his original choice that explains both his acceptance of a journey to the *selva* and his choosing to return to civilisation, what original project makes killing the leper, and staying with Rosario impossible for him? In terms of existential psychoanalysis the narrator is not forced, as he himself claims, to abandon a possibly authentic way by his commitment as an artist. He chooses himself as an artist in terms of an original choice—failure?—that excludes remaining in Santa Mónica. In the light of Sartre's insistence on the freedom of the *en-soi*, the last page of the narrator's text in *Los pasos perdidos* would be seen to be just as ironical as the rest of his account. But is it? Here we arrive back from a possible critic's use of Sartre to a possible authorial use: the dividing line between the two has everything to do with the overall meaning we choose for the novel. But even though such an approach is tempting, it will be left aside for the moment.

The narrator—who in spite of his own belief in the importance of naming, remains stubbornly unnamed even while he tells us of Rosario using his name for the first time—is a man of his time in that he uses as commonplaces a number of Sartrean concepts, or concepts that, though found in many writers, form part of the Sartrean approach. The very idea of naming as the prose-writer's function appears in *Qu'est-ce que la littérature?*, though, creating a typical vicious circle, Sartre adds a warning: "L'erreur du réalisme a été de croire que le réel se révélait à la contemplation et que, en conséquence, on en pouvait faire une peinture impartiale. Comment serait-ce possible, puisque la perception même est partiale, puisque, à elle seule, la nomination est déjà modification de l'objet?"[7] Sartre's remark summarizes precisely the problem that Carpentier addressed in *Los pasos perdidos* and with which the narrator can be seen to be wrestling, without much awareness of his difficulties. For the author the attempted resolution at this stage is the first-person technique of *Los pasos perdidos*. For the narrator the problem is more obscure. He assures us that for him "la única tarea . . . oportuna" is "la tarea de Adán poniendo nombres a las cosas" (77). Yet he himself, as if half-aware of Sartre's warning, constantly seeks to evade naming. His tic of using "ciertos", his vagueness about cultural background details, his own anonymity and his avoidance of specifically telling his reader, for instance, of Mouche's lesbian tendencies, all these indicate a fear of the way in which naming modifies the object—a fear that is borne out by his inability to see the jungle except in terms of earlier texts, earlier namings (a "fault" he constantly perceives in Mouche).

But the vocabulary and the conceptual store of the narrator contain many much clearer references to the terminology of post-war existentialism. José G. Sánchez uses the term "inner voices" to refer to these cultural resonances: "Surrealism, Camus' *homme absurde*, and contemporary existentialism are suggested inner voices in the first part of the narrative and, as such, underscore the general sensibility of the period."[8] The word "auténtico", used several times by the narrator, is an obvious example. Though in Sartre's philosophical writings, as in Heidegger, as it is a technical term of ontology, not of ethics, popular existentialism used the word essentially as a moral term and the narrator is no exception. The same confusion is true of popular existentialism as a whole, very much a matter of moral choices, in contrast to the austere claim of *L'Être et le néant* to do no more than clear the way for an ethics that Sartre in fact never wrote. This blurring of Sartre's strict principles came about in a way that clarifies the situation of the narrator.

First, Sartre himself, largely contrary to his own principles in *L'Être et le néant*, drew moral consequences from existentialism in his lecture *L'Existentialisme est un humanisme*, a lecture much more widely read than *L'Être et le néant*, even though Sartre himself later rejected it. Here he seems to use *authenticité* in a much looser sense and gives it a more central place. Secondly, Heidegger too had used *eigentlich* in a way that led easily to moral use of the word. Heidegger's concept of authenticity saw it as a possibility that was denied by *Gerede* and *Neugier*, idle talk and curiosity that was essentially concerned with excitement and distraction. The narrator's moral condemnations of Mouche are partly informed by such ideas—even if in a typical paradox he makes a highly deprecating reference to Heidegger as a Nazi (96).[9] In examining the outlook of the narrator we are dealing, in fact, with a pool of loosely used terms that form the complex of popular post-war existentialism, and not with the strictly-defined philosophical terms of Heidegger or Sartre. For all his disapproval of Mouche, the narrator shares her use of commonplace contemporary "intellectual" language.

Further examples confirm this use of terms without concern for the overall system of thought to which they belong. "Para Rosario no existe la noción de *estar lejos* de algún lugar prestigioso, particularmente propicio a la plenitud de la existencia", reflects the narrator (186). "Plenitud de la existencia" is characteristically Sartrean: his term is "plenitude d'être". Typically, Sartre uses it in a technical way, while the narrator uses it loosely, moralising. Again, the idea of *estar lejos* as being a perception chosen by the mind rather than an objective fact is pure Sartrean phenomenology: "Ainsi faut-il dire que la facticité de ma place ne m'est révélée que dans et par le libre choix que je fais de ma fin. . . . C'est par rapport à mon rêve de voir New-York, qu'il est absurde et douloureux que je vive à Mont-de-Marsan."[10] The narrator's sentence combines two of Sartre's notions in a way that has little to do with Sartre, and inserts them into a context of reflection that contains many elements that are not Sartrean. It should be added that it is here unimportant whether or not Carpentier or his narrator have read *L'Être et le néant*: Sartre serves here to illustrate ideas that were around before his work, and widespread after and largely because of it.

Commonly *L'Être et le néant* made its most powerful impact through the concrete situations that Sartre introduces to develop and support abstract arguments. One of these is the absence of Pierre from a café which the author visits: "Je m'attendais à voir Pierre et mon attente a fait *arriver* l'absence de Pierre comme un événement réel concernant ce café . . .: Pierre absent *hante* ce café . . . ."[11] When the narrator returns to his empty home early in the novel he remarks: "El desorden de la partida presurosa era todavía presencia de la ausente" (13). From this he builds up a picture of an absence that expresses his profound solitude, a solitude that in its way corresponds to the anguished conclusion that Sartre draws from Pierre's absence: "La condition nécessaire pour qu'il soit possible de dire *non*, c'est que le non-être soit une présence perpétuelle, en nous et en dehors de nous, c'est que le néant *hante* l'être."[12] The narrator's account of events and of himself frequently reveals the phenomenological attitude seen in these two examples. Not only does this set the narrator in the historical context which is so important to the novel as a whole, but it also brings into play echoes of the desperate circularity and emptiness of Sartre's world. When Mouche and the narrator make love amidst *muerte* and *angustia* in their besieged hotel we read: "Había algo del frenesí que anima a los amantes de danzas macabras en el afán de estrecharnos más—de llevar mi absorción a un grado de hondura imposible . . ." (58). One is inevitably reminded of Sartre's complex analyses both of the impossibility of love and desire and of the body and sexuality. Similarly the narrator's later thoughts on a couple's need for solitude to avoid "la ironía o la chanza . . . en las trabazones de una pareja que no podía contemplarse a sí misma con ojos ajenos" (105), recalls Sartre both on love and on "le regard d'autrui".

This phenomenological approach permeates much of what the narrator tells us, but since the novel takes the form of a journey of self-discovery, the narrator's relationship to existentialist ideas is not a static, but a developing one. He himself points this out several times: "Ciertas ideas me cansaban, ahora, de tanto haberlas llevado, y sentía un obscuro deseo de decir algo que no fuera lo cotidianamente dicho aquí, allá, por cuantos se consideraban 'al tanto' de cosas que serían negadas, aborrecidas, dentro de quince años" (77). But the language of his time binds him to it, and though he may make progress in developing his own vocabulary, he can inevitably not entirely shake off the deeper-rooted preconceptions of his culture. Sub-chapter VI includes a remarkable example of this as it concerns the existentialist complex of ideas. The narrator, wandering in his hotel, suddenly perceives it as absurd, in a long passage that has clearly-marked debts to Kafka, Camus, Sartre and perhaps Borges. Not because Carpentier is "influenced" by these writers, but because the narrator perceives his world in terms of these texts, of these cultural values. For all his talk of authenticity and his gibes at Mouche's dependence on learned values in her cultural judgements, he is bound himself by his reading. His is not a genuine vision of the absurd but a recollection of certain existentialist motifs. This is confirmed by the way the motifs are presented as ideas that come to him as if ready-formed. They express certain aspects of his situation as he sees it, but they also express his "inauthenticity".

Inevitably mention of authenticity leads into the even more treacherous terrain of alienation. The narrator or his society are at different moments in the novel almost as comprehensively alienated as an average American citizen in an analysis by Erich Fromm. In the early parts of the novel the alienation is largely seen as economic: the narrator does not control his work, he does not experience the process by which food is prepared from natural materials, he feels cut off from nature by machines, tourism destroys the genuine experiences of travel. Later we find him alienated from his own childhood, and commenting on the remoteness of death for urban people. And when he returns to New York at the end he paints a shattering picture of the cultural alienation of the people around him, not to mention his own experience of being split into two personalities.[13] Little of this is uniquely existentialist. Indeed, Jorge Rodrigo Ayora has argued persuasively that the alienated vision we are offered derives from the early Marx of the *Economic and Philosophical Manuscripts*.[14] He sees Carpentier as a pioneer in Latin America in this and goes so far as to propose an overall interpretation for *Los pasos perdidos* in early Marxist terms. But in fact the situation is a good deal more complex. For both narrator and author Marx is one important element among many. Indeed, at the more popular level, existentialist and Marxist thought, antagonistic as they may have been on some fronts, are inextricably interwoven. As Lucio Colletti remarks, writing of the embarrassment caused to "official" Marxism by the appearance in the thirties of the *Economic and Philosophical Manuscripts*, "Marx's early works, virtually abandoned by Marxists, were to become a happy hunting-ground for Existentialist and Catholic thinkers, especially in France after the Second World War."[15] In *Qu'est-ce que la littérature?* Sartre refers to the alienation of work, a characteristic early Marxist argument, as an everyday fact. In this respect the Marxist analysis is an essential part of his own views. Beyond this eclecticism it is also important to observe again the distinction between the narrator and the author. The early analysis of economic alienation in *Los pasos perdidos* is given by a man bitterly frustrated in his work, an intellectual moving in a world of fragmented Marxist, surrealist, and existentialist ideas. The analysis at the end is that of a man with a vision of an organic culture who has returned to find himself more deeply frustrated than ever by the broken-down condition of his society. In both cases he analyses the situation in terms of the ideas of that society. The very Marxist concepts that provide, as Ayora splendidly illustrates, such a powerful condemnation of modern society, may themselves be placed in jeopardy by the nature of the narrative. It will be necessary to step back from the narrator to the novel as a whole to judge the author's view.

So far we have seen how the narrator uses some of the commonplaces of his day and milieu. In some of these cases the boundary between narrator and author becomes vague and often we take their points of view to overlap. The Marxist analysis is one example, but Sartre too provides plenty of examples of this situation. A crucial moment in the novel is that at which the narrator finally comes into possession of the musical instruments that are the ostensible object of his expedition. After an extraordinary and romantic account of the perfectly organic nature of the native society he is observing he tells us:

> Al concluir los trueques que me pusieron en posesión de aquel arsenal de cosas creadas por el más noble instinto del hombre, me pareció que entraba en un nuevo ciclo de mi existencia. La misión estaba cumplida. En quince días justos había alcanzado mi objeto de modo realmente laudable, y, orgulloso de ello, palpaba deleitosamente los trofeos del deber cumplido. El rescate de la jarra sonora—pieza magnífica—, era el primer acto excepcional, memorable, que se hubiera inscrito hasta ahora en mi existencia. El objeto crecía en mi propia estimación, ligado a mi destino, aboliendo, en aquel instante, la distancia que me separaba de quien me había confiado esta tarea, y tal vez pensaba en mí ahora, sopesando algún instrumento primitivo con gesto parecido al mío. Permanecí en silencio durante un tiempo que el contenido interior liberó de toda medida. Cuando regresé a la idea de transcurso, con desperezo de durmiente que abre los ojos, me pareció que algo, dentro de mí, había madurado enormemente, manifestándose bajo la forma singular de un gran contrapunto de Palestrina, que resonaba en mi cabeza con la presente majestad de todas sus voces. (181-2)

The narrator is self-analytical, yet the manner of his self-analysis invites the reader to question it. A certain complacency, an awareness that he is destroying the organic life he admires, and the give-away of his unchangeable status as a Western intellectual provided by Palestrina, all these are ironically observed. Similarly the passage contains many words and phrases charged with Sartrean and phenomenological resonances that themselves invite reflection on the true situation underlying the narrator's euphoria. Possession, creation, existence, the "exceptional action" and so on belong to the Marxist-existentialist complex and are used as such by the narrator. These instruments, for him, are the expression of the non-alienated society, of the craftsman and musician who is not *de trop*. He also believes that he is drawing himself out of the undifferentiated "they": he is making himself an individual. But the vocabulary of existence is used as part of a mixture that includes decidedly *passé* words like duty and mission. This mixture in itself helps to suggest the muddled appreciation the narrator has of his situation. And beyond this, some of the resonances of his language and his phenomenological approach rebound against him. In *L'Être et le néant* Sartre wrote: "C'est encore s'approprier . . . que *connaître*. Et c'est pourquoi la recherche scientifique n'est rien d'autre qu'un effort d'appropiation." A little later he writes: "Mais, en outre, dans l'idée même de découverte, de révélation, une idée de jouissance appropriative est incluse." He finds here what he calls the "Actaeon complex": "Le savant est le chasseur qui surprend une nudité blanche et qui la viole de son regard."[16] The narrator's acquisition of the musical instrument is shown up for the destructive act it is by the immediately subsequent criticisms he makes of the absurdity of Fray Pedro's mass in this context, and by his reference to the Conquistadores a page later. The use of the Sartrean term "possession" reveals further layers of irony. For the narrator is a researcher, and a huntsman on a journey. His observation of "primitive" society violates it. His appropriation of its instruments symbolizes the subtler idea that all such research is doomed, since to find out is to destroy. Later in the novel his journey fails for other reasons, but here already, at a moment of apparent success, the inner contradictions of his enterprise appear. If *El reino de este mundo* exemplified Carpentier's theory of *lo real maravilloso* as an inside view, then *Los pasos perdidos* here suggests the ultimate impossibility of such a view. "Voir c'est *déflorer.*" The narrator's fundamental purpose is to use the Indians, to treat them as objects: this concept of possession and reification of others is a basic one in Sartre's philosophy, as it is in Marx's. It is the reverse of the temptation to allow oneself to become an object, to partake of the *être-en-soi*, a temptation experienced by the narrator when he goes climbing with Fray Pedro: "Me siento invadido por el vértigo de los abismos; sé que si me dejara fascinar por lo que aquí veo, mundo de lo prenatal, de lo que existía cuando no había ojos, acabaría por arrojarme, por hundirme, en este tremendo espesor de hojas que desaparecerán del planeta, un día, sin haber sido nombradas, sin haber sido recreadas por la Palabra" (213). Violation by naming, and the loss that is entailed by not naming are two arcs of the vicious circle in which we see the narrator trapped.

The same Fray Pedro is also the occasion for another of the narrator's existential reflections. The incident concerned is given us by the author, but the narrator collaborates in treating it as illustrating his views. Near the end of the novel he hears that Fray Pedro has been killed by savage Indians. Fray Pedro has acted out his beliefs in going to preach to these dangerous Indians and the narrator adds his admiration of this commitment in terms that sound very like Heidegger: "Fray Pedro de Henestrosa había tenido la suprema merced que el hombre puede otorgarse a sí mismo: la de salir al encuentro de su propia muerte" (271). Typically the comment then switches to a quite different scheme of values by suggesting that Fray Pedro has defeated death—the narrator's own version, perhaps, of Christian existentialism.

Such references, often confused, or vague, or self-contradictory are used by Carpentier to allow his hero to reveal his predicament in its full cultural and emotional complexity. On other occasions Carpentier seems to be using them to provide commentary on that predicament from within the narrative but without the narrator being so clearly responsible for them. Naturally we are here dealing with incidents rather than vocabulary. One of the clearest examples is the use of Sartre's famous "look". In *L'Être et le néant*, in one of those illustrations that overshadow the technical conclusions flowing

from them, Sartre depicts a man watching through a key-hole. Suddenly
he becomes aware of being watched himself and the look of the other induces
feelings of shame, of consciousness of himself in a new way. This shame can
only be dealt with through bad faith. There are two crucial passages in
Los pasos perdidos involving "le regard"; the first occurs when Fray Pedro
has first told the narrator of the savage Indians that later kill him:

> Creo que, en aquel instante, me permití alguna burlona consideración
> sobre la inutilidad de aventurarse en tan ingratos parajes. En res-
> puesta, dos ojos grises, inmensamente tristes, se fijaron en mí de
> manera singular, con una expresión a la vez tan intensa y resignada,
> que me sentí desconcertado, preguntándome si les había causado
> algún enojo, aunque sin hallar los motivos del tan enojo. Todavía
> veo el semblante arrugado del capuchino, su larga barba enmarañada,
> sus orejas llenas de pelos, sus sienes de venas pintadas en azul, como
> algo que hubiera dejado de pertenecerle y de ser carne de su persona:
> su persona, en aquel momento, eran esas pupilas viejas, algo enroje-
> cidas por una conjuntivitis crónica, que miraban, como hechas de un
> esmalte empañado, a la vez dentro y fuera de sí mismas. (214)

The narrator experiences a sense of shame, of being observed, pinned
down, exposed, but immediately a movement of bad faith protects him from
his own shame as he assures himself he cannot see how he has annoyed the
priest. The whole passage is informed by Sartre's long and complex analysis
of the situation and thus is linked to the major themes of the novel. For
instance:

> La pudeur et, en particulier, la crainte d'être surpris en état de nudité
> ne sont qu'une spécification symbolique de la honte originelle: le
> corps symbolise ici notre objectité sans défense. Se vêtir, c'est dis-
> simuler son objectité, c'est réclamer le droit de voir sans être vu,
> c'est-à-dire d'être pur sujet. C'est pourquoi le symbole biblique de la
> chute, après le péché originel, c'est le fait qu' Adam et Eve "connais-
> sent qu'ils sont nus". La réaction à la honte consistera justement à
> saisir comme objet celui qui saisissait *ma* propre objectité.[17]

Shame is awareness of oneself as an object, bad faith is a dressing-up of
one's nakedness. A major characteristic of the "paradise" that the narrator
discovers, where he and Rosario play at Adam and Eve, is the confident and
natural nakedness they find themselves able to adopt. Superimposed on
the Biblical paradise is a "Sartrean" paradise where ordinary human limitations are radically escaped. The look of Fray Pedro reveals why such an
escape cannot be sustained. For after the first movement of bad faith the
narrator adopts a second defence: he returns Fray Pedro's gaze and sees
only eyes. He is responding as Sartre suggests in the last sentence of the
passage above by turning Fray Pedro into an object. In a later passage
Sartre takes this up again: "Mais un regard ne se peut regarder: dès que je
regarde vers le regard, il s'évanouit, je ne vois plus que des yeux."[18] Thus
relations between individuals are doomed always to collapse into subject-
object relationships, the profound cause perhaps of the narrator's failure to
achieve a permanent relationship with Rosario. The look of the other not

only reveals oneself as an object but also fixes one in time and space.[19] The narrator's aim is to escape time and lose his "civilised" sense of space. Yet Fray Pedro's look serves to reveal that to be seen is to be placed without appeal in both time and place: another reason for the narrator to try to avoid the priest's look, to retreat into a self-serving bad faith. "Mon souci constant est donc de contenir autrui dans son objectivité et mes rapports avec autrui-objet sont faits essentiellement de ruses destinées à le faire rester objet."[20] Fray Pedro momentarily does to the narrator what we earlier saw the narrator do to the Indians he wished to study by appropriating their instruments and observing them. The duality clothed-unclothed serves perfectly to illustrate the impossible situation of the "civilised" man trying to enter into or learn from the "primitive" man.

The other important look is that of the leper Nicasio. Again it is the eyes that are emphasised: even the eyes of Nicasio, guilty of a terrible crime, serve to make the narrator aware of himself. This time it is a different aspect of the look that is brought into play, for the narrator's self-awareness makes it impossible for him to pull the trigger. Indeed it remains for Marcos to shoot to destroy the face that looks (as the Indians later destroy Fray Pedro's face), to establish himself as a man ultimately worthy of Rosario. "Era Marcos, ahora, quien llevaba el fusil" (239). The whole episode involves a moral decision of an existentialist character, but the details serve to link it with other themes and episodes. In particular, Nicasio and Fray Pedro are linked through the theme of the destroyed face and eyes: they present to the narrator, in their opposite ways, the face of commitment and action from which he turns away. The episode is informed by Sartre's terminology and views in another way also. At its heart is the refusal of a radical transformation: "Pero una fuerza, en mí, se resistía a hacerlo, como si, a partir del instante en que apretara el gatillo, *algo hubiera de cambiar para siempre.* Hay actos que levantan muros, cipos, deslindes, en una existencia" (238). This accords very closely with Sartre's description in *L'Être et le néant* of radical modifications of one's project, of "l'instant libérateur".[21] For Sartre each one of us chooses himself in his fundamental project. That choice defines us, rather than the choice being determined by some essence or true self: "[Adam] se définit par le choix de ses fins." He goes on to distinguish between reflective and non-reflective decisions. Non-reflective decisions will always be in accord with the fundamental project, while reflective, or voluntary, decisions may appear to be opposed to it. But at a deeper level even voluntary decisions serve the fundamental project. If a man's project is to be inferior he will wish to be a great artist in order to live inferiority. The only escape from the fundamental project is the "instant libérateur", in which the whole project is made past, and a new project chosen. The narrator experiences a "fuerza" in himself that prevents him choosing this fundamental change. Instead he thinks over the appalling decision he has to make at the reflective level where it is in any case impossible to effect a transformation. But the situation is not, as Roberto González Echevarría suggests, that the narrator tries to avoid assuming historicity by not shooting the leper; rather the leper's look reveals his historicity to us.[22] An instant is offered whereby the narrator could escape his time and make another time his, but he fails to seize it. His evasion of the possibility of "conversion" reveals with the utmost clarity not just a failure of commitment but that for all his talk of decisions for a new life, he is basically still the man who was frustrated in New York. The precise nature of the decision-making process here explains why his earlier decision ("Hoy he tomado la gran decisión de no regresar allá") was so superficial and fallible, and raises queries as to the real meaning of that decision.

The narrator's decision to return *allá* by plane is also involved. Carpentier succeeds remarkably in conveying the inevitability of the return in sub-chapter XXXIII, which follows immediately on the narrator's refusal to shoot the leper. Nevertheless on both occasions he makes *decisions* that define and reveal him. In the decision to return, in addition, Sartre's analysis provides a further clue: "La réalité-humaine rencontre partout des résistances et des obstacles qu'elle n'a pas créés; mais ces résistances et ces obstacles n'ont de sens que dans et par le libre choix que la réalité-humaine *est.*"[23] This is the situation of the narrator: he tells us he is forced to return to civilisation for paper, the lack of which is the only obstacle to his remaining at Santa Mónica. But Sartre's presence reminds us that we create our own obstacles by the future that we choose for ourselves. To use his own illustration, a crag is only unclimbable if we choose to see it as something to be climbed. Similarly, it is only from the point of view of the "civilised" composer that a lack of paper is an obstacle. Again he reveals his true project, and at the same time his narrative unreliability. In particular the background concept of existential freedom that is continuously brought to the reader's mind casts doubt upon the way in which from the beginning of the novel, and especially there, the narrator presents himself as a drifter, his life guided by the chance of other people's decisions. This view is correct insofar as his life is "inauthentic" in Heidegger's sense, yet in a Sartrean sense there is a deeper, underlying meaning to this apparent lack of decision-taking.

The narrator's non-decisions, then, turn out to be his real decisions, while his one major decision, to remain in Santa Mónica, is a piece of whistling in the dark. Such a presentation is necessarily over-schematic, but a reading of the pages immediately after the great decision will show the rich and complex irony involved, conveyed in the detail of the writing: the over-emphatic defiance, the hasty excuses-in-advance, the fatal self-consciousness of his actions, his romanticism, his self-justification in terms of the "civilised" literary tradition, including a revealing reference to Ulysses' cruelty in forcibly removing his crew from their happiness in the land of the Lotus-eaters. The tone gives the narrator away, and the vocabulary hints again, among other things, at Sartre's scheme: "Yo, para amarla . . . he tenido que establecer una nueva escala de valores . . ." (207). Values are created by choice, as the narrator claims, but he has precisely not created a new scale of values. The final necessity to return to New York and stay there is seen, as always, to be embedded in his very decision not to return.

From this point of view one can comment on much of his behaviour in other areas. His relationship with Rosario is one of intense happiness, yet it too contains the cause of its eventual destruction by the narrator within itself. She remains an object for him, the affair is always seen exclusively through his subjectivity. When he attempts to understand her point of view his preconceptions are alien to hers and his explanations unsatisfactory as well as over-intellectual. If love is the attempt to overcome the subject-object division, to possess another subjectivity, then the narrator's relationship with Rosario is an inevitable failure, a failure only screened by the narrator's self-deception.

The narrative technique, coupled with the intellectual background, have shown a character in bad faith. The narrator pursues sincerity, pursues authenticity. He strives to be himself, to escape alienation, to enter an integrated and organic world, a world where his identity is established and recognised. All of these ideals are seen to be impossible, for to strive for each is seen as an example of bad faith. All of them make the assumption that there is a true self to be found, an essence that has to be discovered as the key to personal harmony. But if, as Sartre maintained, the essence is only created by the choices one makes, then the search for identity in this self-conscious way is a false trail.

It remains to decide whether the narrator is always in bad faith, or whether by the end of *Los pasos perdidos* he has come to understand his true condition. It is here that Carpentier's eclecticism comes into play. The Sartrean element in the novel is only one among many. Marxist and Freudian strands are present; there are the major themes of music and of anthropology;[24] there are the constant references to the texts of American history; the novel has been interpreted in Jungian terms[25] and González Echevarría sees important remnants of Spengler in it. All these are filtered through the subversive narrative method and magically intertwined, so that no one of them can be offered as the authentic key. But the issue of the possible bad faith of the narrator in the last page or two involves them all. And in a larger context we are faced with the balances drawn between those pairs of opposites that reappear throughout Carpentier's work: the individual and the collective, the particular and the universal, freedom and determinism, a fixed human nature and the possibilities of revolution.

The narrator's final stance is in many ways a curious one. The artist, he tells us, is the only human being "que está impedida de desligarse de las fechas". Indeed he suggests that as the floods abate, the entrance to the world where time is escaped will reappear, to be available, presumably, to men who are not artists. The limited, rather self-indulgent nature of this conclusion seems quite inadequate. The reader, conscious of the vast sweep across the problems of his day that he has just witnessed, is left with a sense of emptiness at this personal conclusion, whose limitations are emphasised by the grandiloquent form it assumes: "Hoy terminaron las vacaciones de Sísifo" (286). This inadequacy can only reflect the inadequacy of the narrator. Don Quixote-like, he presents himself as the man who *now* understands, but his revelations fail to live up to what his rhetoric leads us to expect. The last two pages are a mixture of truths, partial truths, and rationalizations; the reader has to sort them out in the light of what has gone before. Thus the apparent determinism of the narrator's conclusion, reflected in his choice of Sisyphus, is defused, for we ask, as before, what the real project of this "artist" is. Is he an artist, or is he merely setting himself the goal of being one, in order to express something else? Is he bound by his time, or does he choose to see himself as bound by his time? The novel as a whole lays before us these possibilities, opening up a future in which freedom and determination are problematically balanced.

Carpentier never lets the reader forget his presence, whether through his wilful dislocations, or through his implicit commentary on the narrator's tale. On several occasions he has also commented explicitly on his novel, and though we should certainly trust the novel rather than the novelist it is worth recalling one comment here: ". . . el final de mi novela, la moraleja, diríamos, afirma que el hombre para ser hombre y realizarse no puede escapar a su época, aunque se le ofrezcan los medios para tal evasión."[26] The conclusion is generalized to man rather than the artist, but the Sisyphean hopelessness is replaced by a simple restriction on how man is to "realizarse". The narrator's search has been into his own past, he has hoped to discover his identity by travelling backwards. But that implies that identity is given, that there is a real self, that the past exists independently of present perception. It is such ideas that *Los pasos perdidos* undermines, pointing instead to the future. In the earlier *Viaje a la semilla*, for instance, Carpentier had unequivocally turned time backwards to a given, to a seed of the future. In *Los pasos perdidos*, he travels backwards to find one cannot travel backwards, for the narrator has to invent his own journey even to make the attempt. From now on the necessary starting-point will be acceptance of one's existence at a particular point in time. Self-realization can only arise through seizing the freedom of the future, or accepting the "instant libérateur", or creating an identity out of present choices, not past roots. Sartre asserts in *Qu'est-ce que la littérature?* that literature is "le mouvement par lequel, à chaque instant, l'homme se libère de l'histoire."[27] Even writing, in the future, may be an escape-route rather than the strait-jacket that it is in Roberto González Echvarría's nice summary of *Los pasos perdidos*: "Carpentier presenta a un hombre atrapado en una camisa de fuerza: la totalidad sistemática de la cultura occidental. . . . Para el lector la novela

debe ser, pues, una especie de llave que le permita, como un Houdini, escu-
rrirse de la camisa de fuerza en que se ve encerrado junto con el narrador."[28]
This corresponds to the experience of Carpentier himself in writing *Los pasos
perdidos* and choosing for it a first-person narrative method. Houdini-like
he escapes from an earlier literary psoition when he puts into the wretched
Mouche's mouth views that in the preface to *El reino de este mundo* he had
made his own: "Mouche acertó a decir que la vista de aquella ciudad fan-
tasmal aventajaba en misterio, en sugerencia de lo maravilloso, a lo mejor
que hubieran podido imaginar los pintores que más estimaba entre los
modernos" (124). The irony is only heightened by the narrator's comment:
"No eran tontas las observaciones de Mouche." Thus Carpentier distances
himself from "lo real maravilloso" as he distances himself from the narrator
and from the Western cultural complex. It is this radical irony that is the
key to *Los pasos perdidos*, not any particular programme, such as primitivism,
Marxism, organicism, or magical realism. Existentialism is in one sense
privileged in that it is at once part of Western culture and a possible escape
route by its emphasis on the future, but it remains one part of the pattern,
often, as we have seen, serving the irony. *Los pasos perdidos* attempts with
considerable success to hold in balance a large number of themes. It is at
once a powerful criticism of modern society, an analysis of the cultural
situation of the post-war years, a rejection of primitivism, a commentary
on Latin-American writing and on the possibility of fiction, an examination
of the idea of human nature, and an exercise in myth, anthropology, and
history. It uses an extraordinarily large range of sources, interweaving its
material in a way that one can only call magical eclecticism, an eclecticism
that raids the whole of Western culture in the desperate hope of escaping it.

IAN R. MACDONALD

Aberdeen

NOTES

[1] *Los pasos perdidos*, Mexico City: Compañía general de ediciones, 1959, p. 33. Subsequent references will be given in the text.

[2] "Martí y Francia (Primer intento de aproximación a un ensayo posible)", *Casa de
las Américas*, 15, No. 87 (1974), 62-72.

[3] See Roberto González Echevarría, *Alejo Carpentier: The Pilgrim at Home*, Ithaca:
Cornell University Press, 1977, pp. 155 ff., and Klaus Müller-Bergh, *Alejo Carpentier:
Estudio biográfico-crítico*, New York: Las Américas, 1972, pp. 76-78.

[4] "*Los pasos perdidos*. el Azar y la Aventura", *Revista iberoamericana*, 81 (1972),
585-613.

[5] González, "*Los pasos perdidos*", pp. 605-613, and González Echevarría, *Alejo
Carpentier*, pp. 183-6. See also Carlos Santander, "Lo maravilloso en la obra de Alejo
Carpentier", *Atenea*, 159 (1965), rpt. in *Homenaje a Alejo Carpentier*, ed. Helmy F.
Giacoman, New York: Las Américas, 1970, pp. 99-144.

[6] González Echevarría, *Alejo Carpentier*, pp. 158-9. On Sartre and *Los pasos perdidos* see also González, *"Los pasos perdidos"*, esp. pp. 602 ff., Raúl Silva Cáceres, "Una novela de Carpentier", *Mundo nuevo*, No. 17 (1967), pp. 33-37, and Rafael Catalá, "La crisis de la reconciliación y de la transcendencia en *Los pasos perdidos*", in *Cinco aproximaciones a la narrativa hispanoamericana contemporánea*, ed. Gladys Zaldívar, Madrid: Playor, 1977, pp. 83-107. The latter is the only study of existentialism in *Los pasos perdidos*, but takes no account of the novel's narrative irony.

[7] *Qu'est-ce que la littérature?* Paris: Gallimard, 1948, p. 77.

[8] " Carpentier's *Los pasos perdidos*: A Middle Ground View", *Texas Quarterly*, 18, i (1975), 32-48.

[9] See Martin Heidegger, *Being and Time*, trans. John Macquarrie and Edward Robinson, Oxford: Blackwell, 1967, pp. 211-218.

[10] *L'Être et le néant*, Paris: Gallimard, 1943, pp. 574-5.

[11] *L'Être*, p. 45.

[12] *L'Être*, pp. 46-7.

[13] On alienation in *Los pasos perdidos* see M. Ian Adams, *Three authors of alienation*, Austin: University of Texas Press, 1975.

[14] " La alienación Marxista en 'Los pasos perdidos' de Carpentier", *Hispania*, 57 (1974), 886-92.

[15] In his Introduction to Karl Marx, *Early Writings*, Harmondsworth: Penguin, 1975, p. 17.

[16] *L'Être*. pp. 666-7.

[17] *L'Être*, p. 349.

[18] *L'Être*, p. 448.

[19] *L'Être*, p. 325.

[20] *L'Être*, p. 358.

[21] See *L'Être*, pp. 544-55.

[22] "The Parting of the Waters", *Diacritics*, 4, iv (1974), 8-17.

[23] *L'Être*, pp. 569-70.

[24] There are uncanny parallels with Lévi-Strauss's *Tristes tropiques*, first published in 1955, two years after *Los pasos perdidos*. See González Echevarría, "The Parting of the Waters", p. 15, and Sánchez, "Carpentier's *Los pasos perdidos*", p. 42.

[25] Waldo Ross, "Alejo Carpentier o sobre la metamorfosis del tiempo", in *Actas del tercer congreso internacional de Hispanistas*, ed. Carlos H. Magis, Mexico City: Colegio de México, 1970, pp. 753-64.

[26] Quoted by Roberto González Echevarría in "Ironía y estilo en *Los pasos perdidos*, de Alejo Carpentier", in *Asedios a Carpentier*, ed. Klaus Müller-Bergh, Santiago, Chile: Ed. Universitaria, 1972, pp. 134-45. See p. 223. Agreeing with González Echevarría's argument in his book that Carpentier's remarks are commonly at variance with his practice, I have deliberately avoided mention of C.'s many references to Sartre in his non-fictional writing.

[27] *Qu'est-ce que* . . ., p. 132.

[28] "Ironía y estilo", p. 139.

II

EL OBSCENO PÁJARO DE LA NOCHE:
A WILLED PROCESS OF EVASION

The Chilean novelist José Donoso's *El obsceno pájaro de la noche*[1] is a novel of considerable complexity and, it seems to me, great originality.[2] Its obscurity and the many problems which impede any *comprehensive* interpretation are unusual, even in an age of obscure and difficult literature, and it is my contention that the motivation behind the confusion and contradictions of the narrative may well be unique. Needless to say, not all the striking features found in this novel are without precedent; this is not the first time that an author has dealt with monsters (perhaps "freaks" would be a better translation); a narrator who is mentally incapable is not entirely new and, on a narrative level, we can go back as far as Boccaccio for a tale of a man who pretends to be deaf and dumb in order to gain admission to a convent.[3] Even the confusion of the reader by a narrator who is deliberately deceptive, rather than just unreliable, is not unknown to us, as Wayne C. Booth has pointed out.[4] But Donoso's great originality lies in the mutually exclusive "facts" which form a complicated network in this novel and in the origins of the peculiar inner logic which runs through their presentation and which it is the purpose of this article to reveal.

El obsceno pájaro de la noche is a kind of autobiography. In spite of so many contradictions and the virtual impenetrability of the narrative, most critics seem to agree with Hernán Vidal that the "diversas voces narrativas" of the work are no more than "máscaras adoptadas por *un* foco de conciencia",[5] and that this "foco de conciencia" is Humberto Peñaloza, who later becomes el Mudito. Whether it is possible to see the text as symbolically autobiographical on the levels of the "implied author", to use Booth's term, and of Donoso himself is, of course, another question; for the moment we are concerned with the *yo* of *El obsceno pájaro de la noche*, the surface "autobiographer", and there is little doubt that his tale is built around many of the standard and even some of the less obvious motives for writing about oneself that James Olney considers in his brilliant study *Metaphors of Self*.[6] There are two main ones. First, there is the hope of self-knowledge. The narrator, the pathetic old odd-job man at the Casa de Ejercicios Espirituales de la Encarnación de la Chimba, a hospice for unwanted old women, the forgotten ex-servants of the best Santiago families, looks back on his life and its eternal obsessive need to "be somebody", a phrase that we normally use metaphorically but which, like so many others in this novel, has been extended into literalness. "Mi padre," says el Mudito, "me aseguró que no tenía rostro y no era nadie" (433). How can he become who he is, to say nothing of knowing himself? The second, and hardly less obvious link with conventional autobiography is the novel's apologetic, exculpatory tone. The narrator portrays himself as a pitiful character, from the very beginning— "flaco y enclenque" (14), a "pobre hombrecito" (16)—right through to his affecting, terrible annihilation. His literary talents, as Humberto Peñaloza, never came to anything, but this was through no fault of his: when he started to write, he suffered unbearable stomach pains. His administrative ability in the Rinconada, the closed world of freaks established by his employer and patron, don Jerónimo de Azcoitía, was not appreciated by its inhabitants, and they tormented him and laughed at him. He was cultured, but no-one really realised this until after he had disappeared; even then, his good taste was seen as amusing rather than admirable—it was "de pura invención", says Jerónimo (489). His few forceful, even cruel actions—such as his expulsion of two of the Rinconada inhabitants for breaking the rules —were justifiable. He was intelligent and knowledgeable, but debased himself to become the servant of servants. Though originally innocent of any malicious intention towards Iris Mateluna, one of the orphan girls temporarily lodged in the former convent where he lives, she acted brutally towards him. In the end, he is exhausted, ill and terrified, but the old women inmates pursue and torment him, sew him into a sack inside a sack inside a sack and abandon him when they move into a new home. As he tells his tale, he makes it clear that with the exception of one act of hubris—when he told Jerónimo that he was already an author (280)—he has done nothing to deserve his continuous suffering.

If this is "autobiography", the reader soon discovers that it is an odd variation of it. In his *Design and Truth in Autobiography*, Roy Pascal talked about "the numerous ways in which autobiographies are not truthful",[7] and Heine once said, according to Dostoyevsky,[8] that trustworthy autobiographies are almost an impossibility; there is nearly always some measure of falsification, whether intentional or as the result of the narrator's self-deception. But *El obsceno pájaro de la noche* is not just a man trying to present a sympathetic picture of himself or portraying himself as a hero. It is not just arbitrarily obscure or incomprehensibly fantastic either. In it, many pieces of information given to the reader are subsequently contradicted, many of the events recounted are then said not to have happened, there are conversations which may or may not have taken place and characters are themselves then someone else, or themselves *and* someone else. What the reader believes, on a narrative level, is up to him, and bearing this in mind, it is difficult to guess what criteria have led so many critics to acceptance or rejection of various "facts" in the novel. Hernán Vidal, in his book on Donoso, points out the danger involved in trying to create order out of chaos with this "modelo para armar", since it is an invitation to exercise "el comprometedor privilegio de equivocarse",[9] but himself goes on to claim that, for example, el Mudito *pretends* to be deaf and dumb,[10] that Jerónimo de Azcoitía's patronage of Humberto forms part of one of his hallucinations,[11] that the Rinconada episode is a "ficción total", a kind of "juego lingüístico en que las obsesiones de Peñaloza alcanzan el máximo de posibilidades de metaforización".[12] In fact, to take only the first case, it is impossible to know *from the text* if the Mudito is dumb or not (though Donoso himself has said that he is not):[13] sometimes he can speak and sometimes not. And there is confusion as to whether he is deaf. In one section of the novel, written in the third person, Emperatriz, the "queen" of the Rinconada, refers to him as "sordomudo" (479). In another, the narrator himself reacts to the inaudible conversation of the nursing staff as he lies on his sickbed by asking, apparently horrified: "¿Estoy sordo además de mudo?" (276). His vision of himself at another point is again of a "sordomudo" (298), but here he is imagining the comments of passers-by, and they may be mistaken. It is impossible to know what the truth is. Other critics depend on the veracity of other statements or episodes to support their arguments. One more example will do. José Promis Ojeda, in his ingenious interpretation of the novel in "La desintegración del orden en la novela de José Donoso",[14] sees the key to many of its ambiguities in a conversation that takes place between Inés de Azcoitía, Jerónimo's wife, and her friend Raquel Ruiz on the subject of an ex-secretary of Jerónimo's, "uno como medio enano pero no enano y con el labio leporino mal cosido, y como gibado . . . una calamidad" (395), who was, it seems, Humberto Peñaloza. This "ser deforme", says Promis, projects his own deformities on the world around him while keeping quiet about his own appearance.[15] But did this conversation actually take place? How can we tell? Promis Ojeda himself points out many of the contradictions of the work in this very same article: we have a *niña-bruja* who is also said to be a *niña-santa*; Jerónimo de Azcoitía is single, married and widowed, has one son, is childless, is alive and dead; Iris Mateluna, one of the orphans at the former convent, is a child who has not yet reached puberty, a prostitute, a pregnant woman and a virgin mother; el Mudito himself is Humberto Peñaloza, son of a primary school teacher, secretary to Jerónimo de Azcoitía, a dumb beggar, a foundling brought up in the Casa de Ejercicios Espirituales and an orphan who spent his childhood with a series of beggars who found his pitiful looks good for business. He is now, we must add, dumb, deaf and dumb, neither deaf nor dumb; he has slept with Inés de Azcoitía and he has not; he has written a book, and he has not; he has had intercourse with Iris Mateluna and yet, perhaps, he has not. Jerónimo's son, if he had a son, was incarcerated in a world of monstrous freaks, where his dreadful deformities seemed normal. His mother, Inés, died soon after his birth, or perhaps she did not; perhaps, indeed, she was barren and retreated in old age to the Casa, abandoning both Jerónimo and the luxuries of her past life. Jerónimo is both impotent and sexually insatiable. And there are whole episodes that are confusing in the extreme. For example, "Boy"—Jerónimo and Inés's son—once grown up, comes to the police station when Humberto/ el Mudito is arrested for stealing copies of his own book which Jerónimo once acquired by sponsoring its publication;

in a dramatic scene, el Mudito triumphs, proving to Boy that he was the author of the book by writing out the whole of the first chapter from memory, and the police tell him that he is free to go. Then, we are told, one of the policemen adds: "tienes suerte que te soltemos, el futre no pudo venir, telefoneó para decir que lo siente mucho pero que todo es tan insignificante, tan sin importancia, que no vale la pena caminar las dos cuadras desde su casa hasta la comisaría" (166). Boy was not there. Or was he?

It is surely impossible to know how to choose between the various versions of the truth that we are given. Perhaps Francisco Rivera is right when he claims that there is little point in seeing what he calls the book's "magnificent disorder" as a whole;[16] perhaps any critic who attempts to do so deserves John J. Hassett's implied criticism of those who continue to seek in Donoso "features that constitute essential ingredients of the nineteenth-century novel".[17] And yet, a common-sense reaction when faced with two or more conflicting versions of "facts" is certainly a natural one, and the aim of this study is to show that it can, in this case, be fruitful. Some critics have come close to making my point for me: "el narrador nos hace trampa," says Alicia Borinsky;[18] "this is clearly a work intended to confound the reader," claims John Caviglia;[19] we get to know the narrator and his "circunstancia vital", says Hernán Vidal, "según tendencias mentales que la simbolizan, *la distorsionan y la falsifican*" (my italics).[20] The reaction of the ingenuous reader is likely to be that someone is, purely and simply, lying. This, of course, is no answer, since literature is, by definition, "a lie". In what way, we ask, is this novel any different? We must look for a more sophisticated hypothesis in order to reconcile conflicting information. Narrative lying is the *raison d'être* of the novel. We may never find out what the truth was, but we must ask ourselves why it was hidden.

Julio Cortázar's *Rayuela* contains a statement made by his character Morelli which would seem to sum up the accepted view of the motives of a novelist: "en general todo novelista espera de su lector que lo comprenda," he says.[21] Many theorists of the novel have even based classification systems on the various means used by authors to communicate with the reader, to make the reader an accomplice or, at the very worst, to reduce his hostility. Scholes and Kellogg, for example, talk about the difference between authors' allegiance to what will delight the audience and what will instruct the audience in fictional narrative;[22] Wayne C. Booth's "rhetoric of fiction" involves manipulating the reader and winning his approval, for "even the most unconscious and Dionysian of writers succeeds only if he makes us join in the dance".[23] Why should Donoso risk losing his reader's approval with his obvious prevarication? The answer, it seems to me, is that the narrative of *El obsceno pájaro de la noche* is a means of *avoiding* understanding. The superficial "autobiographer", el Mudito, makes a desperate attempt to escape and hide; words are as much a help in this as are the labyrinthine passages of the Casa de Ejercicios Espirituales.

We must start, therefore, from the premise that el Mudito is lying in order to be elusive, and two questions immediately present themselves. Why should he do this? (This, obviously, comes from the ingenuous reader again, since we all react to narrators as persons.)[24] Then, a more sophisticated question, if the audience is constantly being bamboozled, how can the author possibly expect to make us "join in the dance"?

The narrative of *El obsceno pájaro de la noche* covers a period of half a century, more or less, but the actual narration of the events takes place in the last year of el Mudito's life. It is coloured by the emotions of the "auto-biographer" at the moment at which he is writing; that is to say, here all the episodes are recounted by an old, sick and desperate man, whose over-riding emotion is fear. His life has been a frantic quest for identity, and the telling of it is, as in all autobiography, an attempt to make order out of chaos, to find the total self. As Olney says, memory is called upon to integrate "all the old, half-remembered, or perhaps misremembered selves".[25] But the problem is that there seems to be some sort of danger attached to this process; by looking at el Mudito's evasive reactions, we can diagnose the nature of this danger.

R. D. Laing, in *The Divided Self*,[26] describes typical cases of what he calls ontological insecurity:

> The individual in the ordinary circumstance of living may feel more unreal than real; in a literal sense, more dead than alive; precariously differentiated from the rest of the world, so that his identity and autonomy are always in question. He may lack the experience of his own temporal continuity. He may not possess an over-riding sense of personal consistency or cohesiveness. He may feel more insubstantial than substantial, and unable to assume that the stuff he is made of is genuine, good, valuable. And he may feel his self as partially divorced from his body (42).

An ontologically insecure person, we find, "is preoccupied with preserving rather than gratifying himself" (42); he will react to outside stimuli in a different way from normal people, begin to live in a world of his own, become withdrawn. He fears firstly, what Laing calls "engulfment" (in any relationship he may lose his autonomy and identity), then "implosion" (a terror that the world may "crash in and obliterate all identity" [45]) and finally, "petrification and depersonalisation" ("the dread [. . .] of the possibility of turning, *or being turned*, from a live person into a dead thing, into a stone, into a robot, *an automaton*, without personal autonomy of action" [46, my italics]). His main manoeuvre in order to try to "preserve identity under pressure from the dread of engulfment" is isolation (44); the sense of persecution that results from the terror of implosion gives rise to the need to escape and hide; a fear of being "depersonalised" makes him depersonalise others but, even so, he still sees them as a threat to him because of their very existence.

Now all these reactions can be found in the Mudito. (Even his dumbness is a form of isolation: that an ontologically insecure person is said to *seek* isolation might be seen as convincing evidence in support of the theory that he is only pretending to be dumb. If he is deaf too—or at least, thought to be—then he can be seen as being even more alone.) In the Casa, which is a life he tolerates as preferable to the real world, he is sexually isolated: the only man with the one remaining nun, the *viejas* and the orphans. And he actually lives alone there: even Madre Benita does not know his *patio* (68). When he was Humberto Peñaloza in the Rinconada, he had increasingly removed himself from the outside world, letting more and more time pass between visits to his old café cronies and eventually foregoing them all together. He had exaggerated the inevitable distance between himself and the *monstruos* ("Feo . . . feo," says the horribly deformed Boy when asked to describe him [252]), imagining that they were at best mocking him, perhaps plotting against him and, at worst, literally annihilating him. Countless scenes in the novel describe or are based on his willed isolation from other people—either physical, as when he hides in the maze of passages and cells of the Casa (333), and the "engulfing" *viejas*, under Iris's menacing orders, hunt him down (334), or emotional, as in the scene when he listens, ignored, to the *viejas* plotting or suffers as the *monstruos* enjoy themselves:

> . . . oyó desde lejos, cruzando hasta sus oídos desde el otro extremo del parque donde se alzaban los pabellones de los monstruos, el rumor de la música y de . . . sí, sí, eran carcajadas (256).

Then, too, there are many examples of the Mudito's escaping and trying to hide. The series of masks, or identities, adopted by him in the course of the narrative are ineffectual attempts at hiding: each *medallón*, to use Donoso's own word, is at the same time a means of searching for identity and a disguise so that he himself cannot be found, cannot be "grasped". He escapes from being a law student, the pride and joy of his ambitious father, to being a writer. (Of course, it is possible that he does not: this story may not be true. Nevertheless, for the purposes of the exercise, I want to consider everything we are told, however many conflicting versions may exist.) He runs for his life from his job at the Rinconada, escaping from the intolerable pressures of being an author—something which, in fact, he never manages to achieve, as it is "todo en la cabeza, todo" (259)—and from the horrors of dealing with the freaks who have extirpated 80% of his body. He hides in the Casa. (Again, perhaps this is not true. It may be that he *goes back* to the Casa, since he talks about his period in hospital following his stay at the Rinconada as "mi *ausencia* en el hospital mientras me extirpaban el ochenta por ciento" to Madre Benita, the one remaining nun [297]; then, as the moments in which he is speaking to Madre Benita and lying on his hospital bed overlap and the time scale becomes impossible to work out, he adds: "qué ganas tengo de *regresar* a la Casa" [299, my italics]. Earlier [217], he claims to gave gone to the Casa because Inés had ignored his identity when they made love, and also says that he sought refuge there from Peta Ponce, the archetypal predatory old woman [225].) In any case, the frequency of images and episodes concerned with flight based on fear is significant.

The third reaction to ontological insecurity noted by Laing in schizophrenic patients is equally part of the Mudito's approach to life. He reveals a constant tendency towards the depersonalisation of others and at the same time is afraid that he himself is being turned into something less than human. The tendency is in positive evidence in his classification of people into faceless groups: the *viejas* (who are all *brujas*, "iguales e intercambiables" [509]), the *huerfanitas*, the *monstruos*, the servants and the masters, all of whom are interchangeable or, as Antonio Cornejo Polar says, "reversible": "todo es posible de sustitución".[27] Even when grouped together, they still threaten him, though they are less dangerous in that way than as individuals, such as Peta Ponce, the classic *bruja*, Iris, the only orphan individually portrayed by the author, Emperatriz, the most cultured and aristocratic of the Rinconada freaks, Inés, who in her old age is also Peta Ponce, and Jerónimo, the tyrant-master who—according to el Mudito—has planned, schemed and worked for his destruction ("todo, desde el principio . . . ha sido urdido cuidadosamente, paso a paso, con infinita paciencia, encerrándome en su confianza cuando entré a su servicio, haciéndome testigo de su amor para aprisionarme" [288], and "[don Jerónimo] es mi enemigo" [293], till ultimately, he tells Emperatriz and her husband, Dr Azula, that they must get rid of Jerónimo: "todos necesitamos destruirlo" [479]). From a negative point of view, depersonalisation is revealed in the complete absence of affection, to say nothing of love, in the novel. The narrator admires, but hates his employer, Jerónimo de Azcoitía; in René Girard's *Mensonge Romantique et vérité romanesque*,[28] this classic situation is explained. Girard calls it "médiation interne":

> le disciple [who imitates the aims and desires of a model whom he chooses of his own free will], fasciné par son modèle, voit forcément dans l'obstacle mécanique que ce dernier lui oppose la preuve d'une volonté perverse à son égard. Loin de se déclarer vassal fidèle, ce disciple ne songe qu'à répudier les liens de la médiation (19).

Paradoxically, the model's prestige increases and the attitude of the disciple turns into hatred, which is also directed against himself "en raison de l'admiration secrète que recèle sa haine" (19). To borrow secondhand desires and values from an admired figure is a way of believing in oneself, but it is a self-confidence that is obviously without foundation and, because the disciple knows this, it brings in its train "l'envie, la jalousie et la haine impuissante" (46). El Mudito loathes Jerónimo but admires and desires what he stands for; there is no love here, and there never has been. Even when Jerónimo makes it possible for Humberto to realise his ambitions by offering him a job with him and by sponsoring the publication of his book, he is ungrateful and, indeed, downright offensive. When Jerónimo is concerned about Humberto's health, he refuses help and treatment. He fears interest and affection even more than hatred. Then, too, no relationship between the sexes in the novel is based on anything other than calculated self-interest. El Mudito plans and carries out an incredibly complicated ruse to enable him to have intercourse with Iris Mateluna: he hires the great pasteboard head used by a lad who gives out advertisements in the street and who is Iris's lover. It is something he has to do, but not because he has any tender feelings towards the young girl; she is nothing but a "cuerpo infantil y obsceno y mal lavado" (75) which goes about "invadiendo el equilibrio" of his "vacío nocturno" (76). "No estoy enamorado de ti," he says, categorically, "Ni siquiera despiertas en mí una de esas nostalgias aberrantes que los hombres de mi edad sienten con la proximidad de una vida joven: eres un ser inferior, Iris Mateluna, un trozo de existencia primaria que rodea a un útero reproductor tan central a tu persona que todo el resto de tu ser es cáscara supérflua" (76). The story of Jerónimo and his wife Inés is scarcely touched by any idea of love either. Admittedly, we find that Jerónimo *"se enamoró* de la muchacha más linda e inocente que por entonces bailaba en los salones, una prima lejana con muchas abuelas Azcoitía" (177), but the style of this passage is obviously cynical, even censorious, with its implications of social acceptability: "sucedió lo que tenía que suceder, lo que el ritual de los poderosos exigía que sucediera" (177). Even when we are told that Inés *"lo amó* desde el primer instante" (178), we are not convinced, and in fact the relationship has broken down before they are married. On their wedding night, Inés blackmails her husband, refusing to sleep with him until he has given in to her demands. It is, perhaps, not all that surprising to discover that el Mudito is not in love with the adolescent *huérfana* Iris, and that he is merely dependent on her to carry through some convoluted plot and to keep his secrets. Maybe, too, even the lack of tenderness in the Jerónimo-Inés marriage is not to be wondered at—"suitable" marriages are not always made in heaven—but the lack of love in the relationship which ostensibly motivates the narrator through most of his life, his obsession with Inés, might well be seen as paradoxical and puzzling, unless we bear in mind why he admires and desires her in the first place. As Jerónimo's wife, she is bound to be the object of his affections. He wants to be, or *is*, Jerónimo: they are interchangeable, and their possessions must be shared. At the same time, his desire for her is, as Girard would say, "triangular", not spontaneous, and he cannot really love her: "tout ce qui vient de ce médiateur [in this case, Jerónimo] est systématiqument déprécié" (20). Furthermore, claims Girard convincingly, there has to be disappointment in any kind of apparent fulfilment: if he is truly satisfied and content, a man who hates himself will have to find some other inaccessible object for his desires so that he can enjoy his degradation. Humberto/ el Mudito does not love Inés, but he is dependent on her for part of the functioning of his being, such as it is.

In *El obsceno pájaro de la noche*, all relationships normally founded on love and affection are based on self-interest.[29] Everyone uses everyone else for their own purposes. (In Donoso's next book, *Tres novelitas burguesas*,[30] this idea is taken to its logical conclusion as people dismantle and reassemble each other in the nightmare elegance of fashionable Barcelona.) Donoso himself has pointed out that "where there is love, there cannot be dependence", and he adds that his characters "don't love because they are mostly dependent".[31] In this atmosphere of hostility, it is evident that those individuals who escape from the relative security—as far as the self-styled victim is concerned—of depersonalised groups can never be considered as harmless enough to be accepted as true individuals. In what is probably the only moment of fleeting happiness for el Mudito in the entire book, the moment in which he is sure that he did sleep with Inés, he still cannot resist the temptation of seeing her as a symbol, something safer than a person: "Toqué lo prohibido" (295).

Depersonalisation works both ways, we are told, and fear of it is one of the narrator's most striking characteristics. In his series of metamorphoses, he fails signally to fulfil his ambition of becoming a complete person, independent and well-adjusted; he never acquires what a normal baby achieves, according to Laing, as he grows, "a sense of being an entity, with continuity in time and a location in space" (41). And the incomplete character that he is is further diminished by others, with the operation, or blood transfusion, that he undergoes representing the extreme form of this plunder. The medical staff—who are actually, he is convinced, the *monstruos*, "disfrazados de enfermeros con delantales y con mascarillas que no ocultan sus monstruosidades" (271)—are taking away his blood, and with it, his individuality. By donating their own blood, they manage to replace his healthy limbs and organs with theirs. Ultimately, it is not just his normality that is diminished, but his very body: he hears someone say that they have "extirpado el ochenta por ciento" (277), and knows that to all intents and purposes he has been "despojado de todo" (296). Furthermore, one of the significant aspects of his claiming to be, or becoming, Iris's miraculous Christlike baby is his increasing inability to do things for himself and his lack of control over his own actions. It is a kind of deterioration, like that of the *viejas* as they wait for death; indeed, he doubtless includes himself when he talks about the inhabitants of the Casa: "aquí todos tienen su propia cara deteriorándose en el orden de un tiempo lineal" (303). In his case, it is a backward journey: from being only 20% of his former self, he is reduced to being "casi todo guagua" (518): his nose runs, he becomes incontinent, he has more and more done for him and, eventually, to him. His strength decreases; his face is no more than a "máscara desprovista de facciones que nadie se ha preocupado en repintar" (331); he is getting smaller (some of the baby clothes he is to be dressed in are still too small, but he will grow into them: "cuando me vaya encogiendo Inés me las irá regalando, y a medida que el porcentaje que queda de mí se reduzca me sentaré en esas sillitas de miniatura, dormiré en esas camas de cartulina dorada adentro del chalet suizo, donde la Iris me criará" [448-9]); they wrap him in intolerably tight swaddling clothes. When Inés, now old and repulsive, wins the "baby" from Iris, he has lost any autonomy he might have had. He is almost non-existent, like a "fluctuante mancha de humedad en la pared" (465); Iris castrates him; he is sewn up in sack after sack and abandoned, then thrown onto a bonfire by an old beggar woman. The wind scatters his ashes. He has been depersonalised indeed.

El Mudito's life story—or, more accurately, what he tells us—is a series of symptoms of schizophrenic ontological insecurity, for it is not just a question of these three main fears and their respective antidotes. We have already seen that the individual feels more unreal than real in the world. El Mudito is constantly in this state, "ni vivo ni muerto" (333), in a condition that Laing describes as "life without being alive" (40), and which is represented in Donoso by a chain of crepuscular images as well as in explicit statements and descriptions of semi-conscious states. El Mudito cannot live because he is "atado a una cama" in a "penumbra que no es ni vida ni muerte" (288), "hundido en este crepúsculo" (289).

Then there is the insecure patient's inability to realise that he is separate from everyone else. One person cannot, of course, be another, love for another, die for another. But el Mudito can. He wants to be Jerónimo de Azcoitía, and he becomes Jerónimo de Azcoitía. When Jerónimo is in danger from a hostile crowd during an election campaign, Humberto takes his place, indeed *becomes* his employer; in doing this, he thinks that he is gradually acquiring individuality. He could have caused Jerónimo's death, he says, but adds: "¿Pero, y yo, entonces? ¿Qué sería de las facciones aún tan precarias que iba adquiriendo mi rostro?" "Todas mis posibilidades de participar en el ser de don Jerónimo de Azcoitía" would have been lost (203-4). Instead, a thousand eyes witness the "fact" that he is Jerónimo; he is shot in the arm, but it is Jerónimo who wears his bloodstained bandage. They have become interchangeable. Just before Humberto goes to her room to make love to Inés, he is convinced that she knows this too: "él me robó mi herida, e Inés, al despedirse de mí en la puerta de mi dormitorio, me lo dijo sin decírmelo: tú eres él" (215). At the same time, seeing Jerónimo as a father figure, he wants to be his son, so that he and Boy become, in a way, one and the same.[32]

An extension to this personal interchangeability with others on the Mudito's part (and these are but two examples of it) is the instability of the individuality of the rest of the characters in the story; Inés and Peta Ponce, Inés and Iris, the *niña-beata* and the *niña-bruja* of the legend that runs through the novel, Raquel Ruiz and her servant Brígida, are among those confused with each other. Laing's "actual possibilities within the structure of human relatedness" (53) are transgressed; the reader is told something that, on the most simplistic level, is not true.

Yet another characteristic shared by el Mudito and many ontologically insecure patients is the need to make sporadic forays into the outside world before withdrawing again into isolation. Although he has this need, el Mudito is, paradoxically, agoraphobic, but again, this is not an unknown symptom in these cases. One which Laing refers to specifically (54) concerns a patient who felt an obsessive need to be important and significant to someone else. ("Qué tipo tan insignificante," says Emperatriz of el Mudito [479]). He is often conscious, too, of feeling "unembodied", in Laing's terminology (65), of being apart from his body: "a mí me guiña un ojo y yo le guiño el ojo del Mudito" (27), for example, or, illustrating the classic hyperconsciousness of the unembodied self, the state of imagined superior knowledge and power which has nothing to do with the weakness or impotence of the body:

> Yo muevo apenas la cabeza. Tengo los ojos opacos. Sigues de largo después de quitar tu mano de mi brazo tullido por las vendas, mi cuerpo agotado por mis correrías en la noche, si supieras, Inés, si supieras lo que yo sé y que no quiero decirte, no puedo decírtelo porque me tiene tullido y agotado . . . (391)

The terror that accompanies this condition is that of complete annihilation, and this is the emotion that motivates all that el Mudito does and says, or says that he does. Each metamorphosis is an attempt to survive, and each attempt is a step towards definitive failure: "being somebody" is a far subtler concept than Vidal suggests when he sees this novel as one of "resentimiento social":[33] in fact, its "realidad más genuina" is fear of dissolution. And yet, having said that, an odd paradox presents itself: among the contradictions of El obsceno pájaro de la noche is the obvious one between, on the one hand, the superficial "autobiographer"'s search for individuality and, on the other, his frantic attempts to rub out what identity he has. He works towards the state that he most fears, as horrified by the thought that death may be denied him as he is by its proximity. Is it possible to reconcile the simultaneous needs for life and for death, for air and for asphyxiating enclosure, for power and influence and, at the same time, for the security of being turned into an imbunche, a creature "con los ojos cosidos, el sexo cosido, el culo cosido, la boca, las narices, los oídos, todo cosido" (41)? How can el Mudito say: "Déjame tranquilo, déjame anularme, deja que las viejas bondadosas me fajen, quiero ser un imbunche metido adentro del saco de su propia piel, despojado de la capacidad de moverme y de desear y de oír y de leer y de escribir, o de recordar" (433) if the search for existence is the reality behind the narrative?

The answer is based on the perverse logic observed in schizophrenic patients over a period of many years, especially in suicides. Dr Otto Rank comments on it, though here he is referring to some literary heroes:

> entre le suicide auquel recoururent ces héros et la crainte de la mort [. . .] il n'y a qu'une contradiction apparente [. . .] on voit que le suicide est autant une manifestation de leur crainte de mourir que

de leur disposition au narcissisme; [. . .] ces héros et leurs auteurs [for several of the authors he is considering themselves committed suicide] ne craignent pas la mort: ce qui leur est insupportable, c'est l'attente de leur sort inévitable. [. . .] La pensée normalement inconsciente de la destruction du Moi (le meilleur exemple du refoulement d'une notion insupportable) martyrise ces malheureux en leur représentant leur disparition complète pour toute éternité. Seule la mort peut les débarrasser de ce martyre. Ainsi s'explique le fait paradoxal que pour se débarrasser d'une angoisse insupportable de mourir on se précipite volontiers dans la mort.[34]

It is a question of dying so as not to die. In Dostoyevsky's *The Possessed*, Kirilov kills himself to end an existence "threatened with tomorrow's zero".[35] In Hannah Green's chronicle of a young schizophrenic patient, *I Never Promised You a Rose Garden*, the psychiatrist tells of an ex-patient who used to practise the most horrible tortures on himself. When asked why he did such things, he said, "Why, before the world does them". Here, too, we find "the surprise of the inevitable", with all its horrors.[36] Suicide and self torture have become positive acts. Laing puts it like this:

It seems to be a general law that at some point those very dangers most dreaded can themselves be encompassed to forestall their actual occurrence. Thus, to forego one's autonomy becomes the means of secretly safeguarding it (51).

This attitude is manifest in *El obsceno pájaro de la noche* not only in the ultimate self-annihilation of the Mudito, but also in aspects of his way of life, for example, his sealing up of doors and windows in the Cosa: "las ventanas que he ido sellando para que no las destruyan" (373). Instead of the narrator's false selves serving as embryos for the acquisition of personal identity, they start to destroy him—the masks are wearing him ("Él los había inventado a ellos, no ellos a él," he complains [255]; "A veces pienso . . ." says Emperatriz, "sí, pienso que yo lo inventé a él [Humberto] tal como él soñó este mundo [the Rinconada] en que nos tiene cautivos" [412]; "Tengo que eliminarte," says el Mudito to Jerónimo, "Mi imaginación es tu esclava" [471]) and he has to escape. One possibility is almost catatonic withdrawal—to dumbness and isolation in the Mudito's case. The other, the last resort, when no-one can even see you ("ni me miran los ojos cuando me dan mi papilla" [522]), is—to use Tillich's phrase—"avoiding non-being by avoiding being".[37] Nothing has worked; he cannot, says Laing aptly, "regain his foothold 'in' life again *by the simple repetition of his name*" (111, my italics). The game, like all the games in the *Obsceno pájaro*, has got out of hand.

This, then, is Donoso's originality: the narrator is telling his story so that he will *not* be understood. It is a process of evasion, not self-revelation. "To be understood correctly is to be engulfed," says Laing, "to be enclosed, swallowed up, drowned, eaten up, smothered, stifled in or by another person's supposed all-embracing comprehension. It is lonely and painful to be always misunderstood, but there is at least from this point of view a measure of safety in isolation" (45). To keep himself alive, the narrator has to elude the other people in his world, and they include his audience. He hides in the labyrinthine passages of the Casa and in the tangled complexities of his narration. Because of "el horror de lo inevitable" (368) he must use every stratagem at his disposal; he tells us what he is doing in an episode in his story. The father of your coming baby, he says to Iris, is afraid,

> tiene miedo porque lo andan persiguiendo y eso es lo que da más miedo de todo, que a uno lo persigan y uno se inventa motivos y urde dramas en que protagoniza hechos que jamás ocurrieron para justificar ese miedo . . . (341)

It is not without significance that Iris answers: "Ya no te entiendo . . . habla claro . . ."). "Yo hilvano la fábula en tu oído," he goes on, "para salvarme" (343), and refers to "esta [. . .] novela que urdo porque necesito engañarte" (344). The repetition of images is significant too, as when, later, Emperatriz reflects on the agony of having to go out into the world once a year to report on life in the Rinconada to Jerónimo: "esta salida anual para *urdir el laberinto de mentiras sólidas* como viejas paredes de adobe con que enredaba a Jerónimo, mantenerlo lejos de la Rinconada" (406, my italics). Presumably, this technique might actually be successful; at least, the narrator seems to think that others use it successfully. Emperatriz maintains that Humberto fled from the Rinconada when he realised that "todo, en realidad, era incontrolable. O incontrolable para él, porque, para decir la verdad, ella, Emperatriz, a su manera, lo controlaba y lo había controlado durante más de diez años: con mentiras" (409). But the complexity of this passage, like so many others, is daunting. In it, Emperatriz gives us her opinion of Humberto and admits to her own deceitfulness; at the same time, we know—as far as we know anything—that it is Humberto, or at least, el Mudito, who is telling us this. It is *his* view of Emperatriz, and *his* view of her view of him. And the whole of the Rinconada episode may well be a complete fiction anyway, as Vidal claims, even within the fiction that is the novel. When Emperatriz says, categorically, that "Humberto era un mentiroso" (410), we are lost: a liar is telling us that someone he may have invented is telling us that he is a liar. It is too complicated for any "threatening" reader, especially since to be a *mentiroso* one must occasionally tell the truth. But in spite of the security of the confusion created and the apparent success of others who use the same technique, the narrator does not feel himself to be safe; everything is *incontrolable*; he must die so as not to die, eliminate himself, bring his story to a close and, by a tragic irony, finally become what he was intended to be: nothing.

Alfred J. MacAdam[38] sees the novel as a satire of "the literary work of art in action, a grotesque work-in-progress that fights to stay alive as it seeks to destroy itself"; the speaking mute is the text itself, and "the life of the narrative depends on the weaving of more and more variations, or on the repetition of these variations". It is an interpretation that is not necessarily incompatible with my own, but it is one which ignores the essential tragedy of the human dimension of the novel and which fails to take into account the emotional force of the text. The fear of apocalyptic dissolution into non-being is, horrifyingly, proved to be justified: there is no salvation, even by becoming Christ, only postponement of the inevitable. The Church provides no refuge and society is no Garden of Eden, however carefully it is organised in order to exclude pain and suffering. For the narrator, living in the world and relating to it is impossible: life is a state of continuous fear and panic. The idea that being and enlightenment are possessed completely by the dead is an optimistic one, and is disputed by *El obsceno pájaro de la noche*. There is no self-discovery here, no miracle, and death brings not being, but non-being, as the narrator always knew it would in his heart of hearts.

In a way, though, this book is not without its miracle, and that is the fact that the reader remains intensely interested and involved long after it has become obvious that, as MacAdam says, "to tell 'what happens' is virtually impossible".[39] Donoso's masterly capacity for constant, challenging mystification is manifested in the fragmentation of the narrative into the interchangeable metaphors of overlapping stories, each of which carries with it a sense of anticipation of resolution, and is, at the same time, enthralling in itself: the rich man who protects his monstrously deformed son by surrounding him with freaks; the young girl who will have intercourse only with a partner wearing an enormous pasteboard head; a group of old women determined to believe in and hide a virgin birth; a servant whose business sense is such that she becomes enormously rich and whose mistress works for her; a man used by freaks as a regenerating machine for their own grotesque organs and limbs; a rich and aristocratic woman who gives up everything to retire to the squalor of an old women's hospice and who wins what little they possess in games of chance; a *niña-bruja* who becomes a miracle worker and is worthy of beatification; a priest who goes insane and prowls, naked, around a convent; a calculating adolescent girl who blackmails an old man; the adventures of a political candidate in a hostile region; the courtship and marriage of an aristocratic couple; the lifelong love of an insignificant secretary for his employer's wife; the fate of a former convent and its inmates; the activities of two of the ex-residents of a colony of freaks who establish an elegant clinic in Switzerland; the terrorising and persecution of an old man by apparently innocuous and simple old women. Each tale has its own tension, and since the same obsessions link them all, the hope of their individual resolution is replaced by the anticipation of overall causal completion as the individual narratives dissolve into ambiguity. We "join in the dance" because the homogeneity of the emotions behind the novel unifies its disparate sections.

Authors are notoriously unhelpful when talking about their own works, but in the case of José Donoso, we are often enlightened by what he has to say. In an interview with Emir Rodríguez Monegal,[40] he admitted that he really does not know what this novel is about, that it was unplanned, that it is autobiographical "en un sentido [. . .] subterráneo" and that it is "la autobiografía de mis terrores, de mis fantasías". "Escribí esta novela un poco para saber quién soy," he adds, and claims that the book "tiene que ser de esa manera; no puede ser de otra". The author is linked to the narrator in a search for self-knowledge and he also, apparently, shares at least some of his character's obsessions; perhaps it will not come as a surprise, then, to read in Donoso's "Cronología"[41] that as a child, he lived in a large, rambling house with eccentric old aunts, that relatives used to play cards all night, that he was fascinated by an unbalanced cousin; we learn that he was hypochondriac, invented stomach pains that turned out to be real, and developed an ulcer which caused him trouble whenever he tried to write. Most important of all, we find that he has undergone psychoanalysis, that he was kept "despierto sólo a medias, con apenas un poco más de vida que un vegetal", and that ultimately he suffered a spell of complete insanity. This is what he says:

> . . . tuve otra hemorragia de úlcera y me tuvieron que hacer una operación de emergencia. A causa de mi intolerancia a la morfina, pasé varios días enloquecido, con alucinaciones, doble personalidad, paranoia e intentos suicidas. [. . .] los efectos de esta locura demoraron un par de años en desaparecer. [. . .] En un esfuerzo sin pausa durante ocho meses, todavía sufriendo de pesadillas y paranoia, empecé a reescribir desde el principio *El obsceno pájaro de la noche*. El recuerdo de los miles de páginas que ya había escrito dio al material una organización quizá redescubierta tras mi experiencia con la locura.

PAMELA BACARISSE

Aberdeen

NOTES

[1] José Donoso, *El obsceno pájaro de la noche*, Barcelona: Seix Barral, 1970.

[2] In *Review*, New York, Spring 1973, p. 78, Carlos Fuentes, Kurt Vonnegut and Luis Buñuel refer to the novel as "a masterpiece".

[3] *Il Decamerone*, ed. Ottolini, Milan: Ulrico Hoepli, 1960, Terza Giornata, p. 165.

[4] Wayne C. Booth, *The Rhetoric of Fiction*, Chicago and London: University of Chicago Press, 1967, p. 159. (First edition: 1961.)

[5] Hernán Vidal, *José Donoso. Surrealismo y rebelión de los instintos*, Gerona: Aubí, 1972, p. 183.

[6] Princeton: Princeton University Press, 1972.

[7] Cambridge, Mass.: Harvard University Press, 1960, p. ix.

[8] Fyodor Dostoyevsky, *Notes from Underground*, Harmondsworth: Penguin, p. 45. (First edition: 1864.)

[9] Op. cit., p. 182.

[10] Ibid., p. 180.

[11] Ibid., p. 195.

[12] Ibid., p. 210.

[13] "José Donoso: la novela como 'happening'. Una entrevista de Emir Rodríguez Monegal sobre El obsceno pájaro de la noche", Revista iberomericana, 76-77, Pittsburgh, July-December 1971, 517-536.

[14] José Promis Ojeda, "La desintegración del orden en la novela de José Donoso", Novelistas hispanoamericanos de hoy, ed. Juan Loveluck, Madrid: Taurus, 1976, pp. 173-196. Also in La novela hispanoamericana. Descubrimiento e invención de América, Valparaíso: Ediciones universitarias, 1973, pp. 205-238.

[15] Ibid., p. 193.

[16] Francisco Rivera, "A Conflict of Themes", Review, New York, Fall 1973, p. 24.

[17] John J. Hassett, "The Obscure Bird of Night", Review, New York, Fall 1973, p. 27.

[18] Alicia Borinsky, "Repeticiones y máscaras: El obsceno pájaro de la noche", Modern Language Notes, 88, Baltimore, 1973, p. 294.

[19] John Caviglia, "Tradition and Monstrosity in El obsceno pájaro de la noche", PMLA, Vol. 93, No. 1, January 1978, p. 33.

[20] Op. cit., p. 183.

[21] Buenos Aires: Editorial Sudamericana, 1966, p. 453. (First edition: 1963.)

[22] Robert Scholes and Robert Kellogg, The Nature of Narrative, New York: Oxford University Press, 1968, pp. 13-14. (First edition: 1966.)

[23] Op. cit., Preface.

[24] Ibid., p. 273. For an interesting discussion of the possibility of the "I" of a text being no more than a grammatical solution, see too Germaine Brée, Narcissus Absconditus. The Problematic Art of Autiobiography in Contemporary France, (The Zaharoff Lecture for 1977-8), Oxford: Clarendon Press, 1978.

[25] Op. cit., p. 264.

[26] Harmondsworth: Penguin, 1972. (First edition: 1960.)

[27] Antonio Cornejo Polar, "El obsceno pájaro de la noche: la reversibilidad de la metáfora", Donoso. La destrucción de un mundo, p. 105.

[28] Paris: Grasset, 1961.

[29] Hernán Vidal furnishes a selfish motive even for Humberto's father's paternal ambitions for his son; he refers to the arribismo of the middle classes: "¡Ser algo! Si no pueden serlo, ¡que lo sean sus hijos!" (op. cit., p. 192).

[30] Barcelona: Seix Barral, 1973.

[31] George R. McMurray, "Interview with José Donoso", Hispania, Vol. 58, Baltimore and Wisconsin, 1975, 391-2.

[32] See Hernán Vidal for theories on this sustitución: op. cit., pp. 202 and 223-232.

[33] Op. cit., p. 180.

[34] Don Juan et Le Double. Études psychanalytiques, trans. Dr S. Lautman, Paris: Petite Bibliothèque Payot, 1973, pp. 106-7. (First edition in French: Paris, Denoël, 1932.)

[35] This quotation is actually from a later work: The Diary of a Writer, trans. Boris Brasol, London and New York, 1949, p. 546.

[36] Hannah Green, I Never Promised You a Rose Garden, London: Pan, 1978, pp. 38 and 65. (First edition: London: Gollancz, 1964.)

[37] Paul Tillich, The Courage to Be, London: Nisbet, 1952, p. 62.

[38] " José Donoso. Endgame", Modern Latin American Narratives. The Dreams of Reason, Chicago and London: University of Chicago Press, 1977, pp. 110-118. Quotations from pp. 113 and 117.

[39] Ibid., p. 115.

[40] See Note 13.

[41] Cuadernos hispanoamericanos, 295, Madrid, January 1975, pp. 5-18.

III

NARRATIVE ARRANGEMENT IN
LA MUERTE DE ARTEMIO CRUZ

The list of books and articles concerned wholly or partly with *La muerte de Artemio Cruz* is already imposing.[1] Prominent among the items included are a certain number which deal directly with the narrative technique. Among these are several of major importance, such as Joseph Sommers, "The Field of Choice: Carlos Fuentes" (Chapter V of his *After the Storm*, Albuquerque, 1968), Nelson Osorio's "Un aspecto de la estructura de *La muerte de Artemio Cruz*", *Nueva narrativa hispanoamericana* (Adelphi University, N. York), 1, 1971, 81-94, also in Giacoman's *Homenaje*, B. Fouques, "El espacio órfico en *La muerte de Artemio Cruz*", *Revista iberoamericana* 91, 1975, 219-48, and more recently a valuable contribution by Hernán Vidal, "El modo narrativo en *La muerte de Artemio Cruz*", *Thesaurus*, 31, 1976, 300-326. But inevitably the interest of critics has tended to centre on the *"yo-tú-él" method* of narration rather than on the arrangement of the incidents, the *dispositio* of the story itself.

Thus Vidal, in his close analysis of the functionality of the method in question is led to refer characteristically to "una *arbitraria* selección de sucesos, personajes y segmentos temporales en la secuencia narrativa" (p. 306) which produces "*violentos* desplazamientos temporales en sentido progresivo y regresivo" and "*arbitrarios* enfoques" (ibid., italics mine) throughout the course of the novel. We have no difficulty in recognizing that behind the adjectives I have ventured to italicize lies the belief that Fuentes was deliberately attempting to convey, through this *fragmentarismo*, a sense of "total incertidumbre ante la realidad" (p. 307). This would be in line with the general reaction against old-style realism and its assumptions about the intelligibility of reality which is typical of the *nueva novela*. It follows that, although for Vidal *La muerte de Artemio Cruz* has an unquestionable "disposición artística" (p. 309), this resides primarily in the superimposition of different strata of perception in the course of Artemio's dying reflections.

Only two writers, so far as I am aware, have seen the question in a different light. One is the distinguished Chilean critic Juan Loveluck in his article "Intención y forma en *La muerte de Artemio Cruz*".[2] In the fourth section, he carefully describes one sequence of the novel, dated 20 May 1919, which is concerned with Artemio's visit to don Gamaliel in Puebla and the circumstances leading to his marriage to Catalina. Loveluck's conclusion is that the conventional chronological order of the episodes has been deliberately rearranged, not so much (as Vidal's article would tend to suggest) in order to convey a message about our perception of reality, as in order to establish a narrative pattern which is "artísticamente más efectivo" (p. 112).

At this stage of Fuentes criticism there can be no question as to the validity of this approach, as compared, for example, with the fiercely partisan judgement of M. P. González,[3] who dismisses the novel's technique as artificial, illogical, "ficticio y contrahecho" (pp. 93-4). If anything is lacking in Loveluck's article, it is that the author does not find space to explain in detail *why*, in his view, the narrative arrangement of the Puebla sequence is more artistically effective than a chronological arrangement. Equally, the question arises whether what is true of that sequence is true of the arrangement of the novel as a whole.

To this question the second writer, Osorio, in his earlier-mentioned article, does not return a fully satisfying answer. Chiefly this is because he tends to identify artistic effectiveness exclusively with clearly-defined thematic correlations and therefore to assume that what constitutes a recognizable link between Artemio's moral abjection and his social success is *ipso facto* all that constitutes the novel's artistry. In my view, what Osorio convincingly demonstrates is that the novel is in fact consciously organized around a given underlying idea. But this is not quite the same thing as showing that it is a successful work of art. For this purpose we need to know in more detail *how* it is so organized. None the less, Osorio's article marks the greatest advance so far in clearing away misconceptions about Fuentes' intentions in the book. My aim here is to try to carry the discussion a stage further.

In order to address ourselves afresh to the problem, we must remind ourselves of the central issue. The novel consists of thirteen fragments of interior monologue in which Artemio is presented in the first person as *yo*; thirteen fragments of response from a deeper level of his personality (according to Fuentes, his subconscious mind),[4] and twelve flash-backs of omniscient narration. It is these last which indicate the time-scale of the story, since the *yo* and *tú* sequences (though they may contain reminiscences) all belong to a relatively short space of time on 10 April 1959, the period just before Artemio's death.

Chronologically the twelve flash-backs run from his birth in 1889 to his death seventy-one years later. Arranged as in a conventional biographical novel the order would be: The actual order, however, is:

			(1959)
(1)	1889	(1)	1941
(2)	1903	(2)	1919
(3)	1913	(3)	1913
(4)	1915	(4)	1924
(5)	1919	(5)	1927
(6)	1924	(6)	1947
(7)	1927	(7)	1915
(8)	1934	(8)	1934
(9)	1939	(9)	1939

(10)	1941		(10)	1955
(11)	1947		(11)	1903
(12)	1955		(12)	1889
	(1959)			(1959)

that is to say, the chronological sequence has been deliberately replaced by a contrasting time order. The question is: why?

If we examine comparatively the two tables of dates we notice a number of interesting features. In regard to the first table we cannot overlook the fact that whereas the last four decades of Artemio's life are regularly allocated two episodes per decade, the period of less than six years from December 1913 to May 1919 (from the battle-scene and death of Regina to Artemio's marriage to Catalina) is allowed three episodes all to itself. The crucial significance of this period is therefore unmistakably apparent, when we consider the episodes chronologically. Passing now to the second table, we can see that two of these episodes remain together not very far from their original position in the chronological sequence (though in reverse time order: 1919 followed by 1913). The third (1915) episode, however, has been transferred to a much later point in the text, in fact, practically to the middle of the novel.

What can we deduce from this? The original fact stands: there are still three episodes relating to less than six years. But one of these episodes has been shifted to become what is in reality the centre of balance of the whole work. If any proof were needed of the unique significance of the October 1915 episode in Perales prison as the basic turning point in Artemio's life. it is to be found here in its deliberate positioning as the central episode. But we can surely go further than this; for to assert that the central episode coincides with the main turning point in Artemio's life and outlook, is simply to continue Osorio's line of argument based on thematic emphasis alone. Of equal if not greater importance is the artistic effect of giving the novel so visible a centre of balance. It should not pass unnoticed in this connection that the October 1915 episode is by a very considerable margin the longest of the *él* sequences which are the spine of the narrative.

Most spontaneously-written novels tend naturally to have an accumulation of incident at the beginning and the end, with a certain relaxation of narrative rhythm in the middle when the original inspiration for the opening has been exhausted and the finale is not yet in sight. So it is that the middle section of novels is often the most structurally revealing part, for it is the test of the author's artistic ability. *La muerte de Artemio Cruz* passes this test with flying colours.

Finally, before leaving the tables of dates, it is as well to mention that if it had been Fuentes' intention to present the main events of Artemio's life as an arbitrary jumble he would presumably have taken care not only to alter the time sequence generally, but also to separate from one another as far as possible the two events usually selected for each decade. In reality, however, we notice that the two events of the 1920's and the two events of the 1930's, though separated by two intercalated episodes concerned with widely-differing periods of Artemio's life, remain none the less contiguous to each other in both cases. The fact that this is not true elsewhere in the novel suggests that here it was intentional and part of a planned arrangement. We shall see how far it is possible to justify this conclusion.

For the moment, we must return to the beginning. Any piece of fiction, viewed as a mechanism, can be seen as the result of a series of choices more or less deliberately made by the author, or as a series of solutions to problems posed by the various requirements of the narrative. The first problem, inevitably, is that posed by the exposition, with its three-fold function of grasping the reader's interest, introducing the principal characters and conveying enough information to make the body of the story intelligible. In a biographical novel such as *La muerte de Artemio Cruz*, the logical and conventional approach is to relate the circumstances of the hero's birth or early life, as Dickens does in *David Copperfield*. When this method of starting the novel off is rejected in favour of another, we are naturally led to consider the reason and to examine carefully what the author has chosen to do instead.

There are two obvious options. One is to select a dramatic incident which will make an exciting beginning, and thereafter supply background information in the form of a summary. Alternatively, the author may decide to emphasise instead some aspect of the novel's thematic content, as Mallea does in the superb evocation of sterility at the opening of *Todo verdor perecerá*, or as Arguedas does in the semi-symbolic visit to Cuzco which Ernesto makes with his father in Chapter One of *Los ríos profundos*. This is in fact the option chosen by Fuentes. Instead of describing Artemio's birth or either of the major dramatic events which he is to be involved in during the Revolution (the battle of 1913 and the Perales episode of 1915), Fuentes first of all shows Artemio at the peak of his "success", surrounded by the fruits (dead sea fruits, as we at once perceive) of his abjection and cowardice.

In other words, the exposition of the novel centres on Artemio's ambiguous achievements in order that the successive episodes, up to that of New Year's Eve 1955, shall gradually fit together to form an ever more cohesive *explanation*: on the one hand of these achievements, and on the other hand of their ambiguity. The New Year's Eve party itself rounds off the central section of the book with marked re-emphasis of the effect created by the exposition. It depicts both the wordly success and its unsatisfying, threatening face in even heavier relief, with all the accumulated impact of what has emerged in between. Thereafter, the remaining two episodes, which, significantly, do not involve the sort of moral choices which are characteristic of the central episodes, constitute a concluding "special effect" with a strong element of indirect commentary designed to stress the relevance of the story as a whole to the history of Mexico.

Already, then, we can perceive three carefully integrated structural principles co-existing in the narrative-organization of *La muerte de Artemio Cruz*. The first and most general principle is based on a simple reversal of time order. The narrative begins with Artemio on his death-bed and at the peak of his outward success, the latter aspect immediately reinforced by the wheeling and dealing of the typical tycoon's day in the opening 1941 episode. The story virtually ends with Artemio's birth. The governing idea here is that of *causal explanation* ("Recordarás y recordarás *por qué*", p. 34,[5] italics mine): a process of working backwards mentally from the achievements via the stages by which they have been brought into being and tracing them to a low point of origin. The aim of the book dictates the method. Inside this over-all principle we perceive another, the second, which, instead of being linear, is circular. Just as the novel begins on Artemio's death-bed and ends with his death, enclosing his life within its circumference, so the main body of the novel begins with success and works round to further emphasis on success in the New Year Party episode. The governing idea in both cases is irony ("toda tu vida habrá contenido y prometido tu muerte", p. 33, along with "Tedio, pero asco, repulsión", p. 225). Finally, a third structural principle, visible in the placing of the 1915 Perales episode, is that of symmetry around a major turning point. Functioning harmoniously together, these three principles produce a taut narrative organization within which the individual episodes are juxtaposed to one another according to a conflictive dialectical pattern which reflects the duality in Artemio himself ("¿Quién no será capaz—como tú—de encarnar al mismo tiempo el bien y el mal?" p. 33). That is to say: on the one hand there is the over-all causal sequence; on the other, in contrast to it, the intercalated episodes of abortive or potential rebellion by Artemio's repressed other self. These last are the main means by which Fuentes prevents his central character from relapsing into total abjection.

The exposition is thus essentially thematic, rather than dramatic. It introduces Artemio, Catalina and Teresa and provides information about their wealth, activities and social standing. But most of all it conveys the ironic contrast between these and Artemio's helplessness, fear and malice, along with the repressed shame and self-disgust which expresses his duality. At the same time the emotional frustration, bitterness and fear of old age felt by Catalina, together with the resentful triviality of Teresa re-emphasise the emptiness of their upper-class life-style. The striking effectiveness of this solution to the problem of the novel's exposition is undeniable. It successfully attaches the reader's interest to the central idea which Fuentes intends to develop in the rest of the book and at the same time manages to fulfil both the other essential requirements of a narrative-opening. It is difficult to see how the same effect could have been created by the more standard procedure of starting with the hero's birth. The choice of technique for the beginning of the novel assumes in retrospect that appearance of inevitability which is the hall-mark of genuine artistry.

The twenty-two-year gap which separates the events of July 1941 from those of May 1919 marks the end of the exposition and the beginning of the story proper. Two glimpses of Artemio's emotional life (3 and 4) are now sandwiched in between two separate but related episodes of his public self-betrayal (2 and 5). Together they form a narrative-unit whose arrangement further underlines the artistic intention governing Fuentes' choice of method. Examination of this arrangement brings the recognition that to have told the story chronologically would have forced Fuentes to sacrifice the extremely successful fictional effect created by the planned juxtaposition of these four episodes. But in addition it would have compelled him to include other material (specifically a description of Artemio's adolescence) which would have further diluted the residual impact the four episodes could have retained if presented at appropriate intervals in time-order. As it is, by dropping the conventional biographical manner, Fuentes is enabled to select his episodes at will and set them in the most artistically functional pattern.

In the Puebla (1919) episode, the two Mexicos: the old, represented by don Gamaliel, and the new, represented by Artemio, meet after the Revolution and join forces. The function of this episode is to explain the background to the picture of Artemio and Catalina's life in 1941 which we have just been given, at both levels: wealth and power on the one hand, frustration and repressed unhappiness on the other. At the same time, the Puebla episode is linked to the central (1915) episode by a common element of symbolism. At the end of Artemio's visit, Catalina releases her caged birds before surrendering herslf to his ambitions: she, that is, remains trapped. Similarly, but more ironically, Artemio is shown trapped in a mine-shaft while attempting to escape from Colonel Zagal. During his period underground he has a day-dream of leading a simple, useful life as a farmer, a dream in which the uncontaminated part of his nature and aspirations is revealed. But his emergence from this apparent trap is in reality the moment of his fall into the real snare, which arises out of his meeting with Gonzalo Bernal in the prison-cell at Perales. This in turn leads directly to the Puebla episode. After this both Catalina and Artemio are trapped together in the same empty marriage, and for the same reason. Each has given up an aspiration of their more authentic selves (Catalina to marry Ramón, Artemio to lead a simple, useful life) without a struggle.

The 1927 episode of political cowardice and opportunism, in which Artemio abandons his former loyalties in order to jump on to the bandwagon of a new, more successful candidate for the presidency, completes the causal sequence which dominates the first half of the novel. While the tycoonery of 1941 is partly explained by the marriage of 1919 and this in turn by the meeting with Gonzalo in 1915, the main thrust of this explanation is economic. The 1927 episode provides the missing political dimension, for as we know from Usigli, "En México todo es política . . . la política es el clima, el aire".[6] We perceive, then, that the method hitherto has been to postpone the crux of the story, the turning point of 1915, until its *consequences* have been widely explored. Thus the Perales episode gradually accumulates more and more significance as we approach it.

But so far we have approached it only from one side, that of the public face of Artemio's existence. The two episodes of 1913 and 1924 which are intercalated into the dominant sequence between the Puebla incident and the presidential election of 1927 relate to the other side of Artemio's story: the emotional aspect. They afford a further example of the same technique of deliberate contrast which was visible in the difference between Artemio's day-dream in the mine and the reality of his behaviour after escaping death at Perales. Essentially, in this case, the contrast is between the end of his romantic dream of love with Regina and the reality of his early marriage to Catalina, together with his first serious lapse into adultery. In both sets of contrasts there is a loss of innocence: a temptation and a fall. Just as Artemio is unable to hold on to his dream of a small farm when a large estate seems to be within his grasp, so he is unable to hold on to his dream of a different emotional world, "otro, soñado, en el que sólo él y su amor tenían derecho a la vida" (p. 73), when the prospect of cementing his power over the Bernal property by marrying Catalina opens in front of him.

The two episodes of 1913 and 1924 are closely related to each other. Both Regina and Catalina are booty of war, victims brutally seized to gratify the victor. In that, and only in that (apart from physical attractiveness), the two women are alike. In all the rest they are deliberately contrasted in a way which is carefully designed to underline the contrast within Artemio himself. Regina is closely associated with the *ventana* symbol which recurs throughout Artemio's reflections. On the other side of the window is the fullness of life, freedom, along with simple everyday pleasures such as are open to all men; what Artemio calls "el perfume de otra tierra" symbolised in the elementary acts of "ver cosas, tocar cosas, oler cosas" (p. 59). Above all Regina is associated with the repressed part of Artemio's self, his spontaneous feelings. But these in turn are seen by him ambivalently. For, while they too are necessarily connected with the fulfilment offered by life on the other side of the window, they are also connected with something else: *awareness*, which is a threat to the selfish "order" ("el orden del hecho recibido", p. 61) which Artemio has deliberately imposed on his life. Hence his reflection: 'Darse cuenta debilita' (p. 61). This ambivalence on Artemio's part explains why the affair with Regina is in itself ambiguous. Kidnapped and raped, Regina succeeds in casting a romantic veil over the circumstances surrounding the beginning of the relationship and, more importantly, succeeds in making Artemio, against the resistance of a great part of himself, join her in the illusion. His raptus after her death is the reaction of a man whose better nature has been betrayed by fate. The end of the idyll fixes irreversibly Artemio's repression of that side of himself, despite a deep longing to recover not only the kind of unconditional love and emotional support which Regina had offered, but also the belief in life's happier possibilities that she had made possible. Alongside "Te amé a ti" must be set "Puedo creer en ti" (p. 60).

If Artemio's relationship with Regina, the spontaneous, uncomplicated "Mujer de la vida, potranca llena de sabor, limpia hada de la sorpresa, mujer sin excusas, sin palabras de justificación" (p. 83) represents an aspiration which is subsequently repressed, his marriage to Catalina is at the opposite pole, with pathos and frustration replacing fulfilment, and with irony instead of idyll. Catalina is the feminine reflection of Artemio's dominant self. His pride finds its match in her pride; his attachment to his own self-centred "orden" is confronted with hers to "el mundo ordenado por don Gamaliel" (p. 103). Above all, both share the same fear of sincerity and self-revelation. In this context their physical enjoyment of sexuality becomes the opposite of what it was in the case of Artemio and Regina: an ironic fact which throws into relief their lack of emotional communication. In the end, instead of holding them together, it forces them apart: Catalina into resentment against herself for surrendering to desire, Artemio to the first of a series of mistresses. Nevertheless, his "plañir interno por algo perdido" (p. 73), the voice of his repressed self, is heard plainly in the words of supplication (p. 114) which he does not dare to outrage his dominant self by uttering. In the context of Catalina's emotional indecision with regard to him, these unspoken words lend the scene a pathos which is absent from the rest of the novel.

The 1913 and 1924 episodes are thus plainly meant to complement each other. But equally they are complementary to the 1919 and 1927 episodes between which they appear. This is clear from the fact that they explain the bitterness and frustration underlying Artemio and Catalina's outward prosperity and prestige in 1941, just as the 1919 and 1927 episodes explain the achievement of these last. The link is made explicit by the phrase in Catalina's interior monologue: "Perdiste tu inocencia en el mundo de afuera. No podrás recuperarla aquí adentro" (p. 113) which locks the four episodes together.

The gap of twenty years between November 1927 and September 1947 marks the transition to the central episodes of the novel: those of 1947, 1915 and 1934. Two features of these are noteworthy. The first is the greater tendency to separate the two aspects of Artemio's life: his public politico-economic career and his private emotional situation, as compared with the narrative-bloc composed of the preceding four episodes. In the 1913 episode, for example, we recognize not only the Regina idyll, but also events of Artemio's military career which lift him out of the common run of young revolutionary officers and begin to put him in a position to bring pressure to bear on don Gamaliel later. Similarly, in the 1924 episode we notice not only the course taken by his early marriage, but also his transition, via the innovations he introduces into the running of don Gamaliel's estates, to a political career. In the three central episodes, however, there is no such overlap. Instead of being causally connected, as hitherto, the two sides of Artemio's life are here dealt with separately. The aim now is to make them reinforce one another mutually at the psychological level.

For the other feature which characterizes the three central episodes is the marked sacrifice of Artemio's character which occurs in them. This forms the real link with the previous set of events. The political, "public" cowardice and opportunism displayed by Artemio in his turncoat action of 1927 is matched by the moral abjection of the Lilia episode twenty years later. But the full force of this last, which merely develops in greater detail the initial adultery of Artemio that rounded off the picture of his early married life, is not felt until we read the much shorter but more memorable description of the end of Artemio's affair with Laura in 1934. The comparison of what Artemio might have secured, in terms of emotional fulfilment, by breaking the grip of his dominant self, with what he eventually settles for with Lilia, forms a perfect frame for the central episode itself, the prison-sequence in Perales. At the same time part of the ambiguity of Artemio's personality disappears in this section of the novel. It is the price which Fuentes has to pay for heightening the emphasis on Artemio's moral insufficiency in order to create a strong centre for the work.

The order of the incidents in the middle of the book is dictated by the double contrast which dominates the beginning of the second half of the story: first between Artemio and Gonzalo Bernal, Catalina's brother, then between Artemio and his son Lorenzo. The essence of the first contrast is contained in the description of Gonzalo as "este nuevo enemigo armado de ideas y ternuras" (p. 197). The very similarity of the two men's positions emphasises this contrast. Both are, intentionally at least, traitors to their class: Gonzalo to the landed oligarchy (cf. his father's comment: "debemos perdonarlo por haberse pasado al enemigo" p. 49), Artemio to the common people from whom he sprang. But they are so for totally opposed reasons, which, in Gonzalo's case, are both intellectual and emotional: "ideas y ternuras". He possesses, that is, ideals which his mind accepts and at the same time, through his wife and child, enjoys a link with a wider society for which the Revolution was originally to have provided a better future. In the case of Artemio there is a deliberate separation of *ideas* and *ternuras* in the three central episodes which is paradoxically designed to re-emphasise their mutual dependence. The core of the main episode of the three, that in Perales, is the discussion by Artemio and Gonzalo of the collapse of the revolutionary ideal because of middle-class timidity and selfishness (p. 195). It brings out the awareness felt by both men of ideological failure. What is different is their reaction. Gonzalo dies, joining the group of those, *el soldado*, Regina, Lorenzo, whose sacrifice, in the face of his own survival, fills

Artemio with so much guilt. Artemio survives, but with an ever-greater consciousness that it is at the expense of those who have died. Faced with what his inner self calls "las dos morales que aquel día te solicitaron" (p. 122), his choice is dictated by self-interest, fear and pride. The comment of his conscience is "temerás el amor, ese día [i.e. when the chance to love arises]" (p. 209).

The two incidents which Fuentes has chosen to frame the Perales episode develop that comment in different ways. The affair with Lilia is specifically devoid of love: "El contrato, tácito, no exigía verdadero amor, ni siquiera una semblanza de interés personal" (p. 152). On this basis it lasts practically a decade. The abortive affair with Laura on the other hand is Artemio's last chance to reach "the world beyond the window" implicit also in the Renoir picture of the girl on the swing (p. 217). It leads from the beginning straight towards love and sacrifice. Once these come into view, he retreats.

The Perales episode and the Laura episode, set side by side with great effect, are in a sense the crux of the book as a whole. As Artemio had been afraid to redeem himself morally in the prison cell, so he is afraid to redeem himself emotionally with Laura. He settles for haunting guilt, obsessive attempts at self-justification (which prevent him, in spite of these three episodes, from losing the last residue of the reader's esteem and changing from an anti-hero to a figure of contempt) and a woman who although "en su poder, comprada por él" (p. 158), nevertheless eludes his total possession and leaves him intimately frustrated. Once more we perceive that the arrangement of this narrative section is perfectly adapted to its function both internal and in relation to the rest of the story.

The usefulness of dividing the novel into groups of episodes from the point of view of their function should not make us overlook the fact that the transitions are carefully prepared. In this way the whole sequence of episodes is locked together into one organically operating entity. Thus, as we have seen, the Puebla episode is causally connected to the 1941 description; the cowardice of the 1947 events is related to the cowardice of Artemio in Laura's flat. Similarly, the Perales episode is linked to the New Year party by the sense of the people waiting to return to the revolutionary struggle (pp. 185 and 277). So, too, the description of Lorenzo's death in 1939, the one incident which stands out quite separately from the others because the él referred to is not Artemio, is slotted into the narrative as a whole by the tú section which precedes the Perales episode. The moment we pause to consider why this particular tú section should have been chosen for the purpose and not any of the others, we perceive at once that the reason is, as ever, an artistic one. It is to point the contrast between the book's basic negative episode: Artemio's refusal to "darlo todo a cambio de nada" (p. 205) and its basic positive one: Lorenzo's readiness to do so. This in turn links Lorenzo to Gonzalo Bernal via the recognition shared by both, but rejected by Artemio, that "hay deberes que es necesario cumplir aunque se sepa de antemano que se va al fracaso" (p. 196). Finally we note that the description of Artemio's ride to and across the river with his son introduces the fact that Lorenzo set out on his last journey to Spain and to ultimate sacrifice, from the very point—Cocuya—from which his father had set out forty years before, towards a sadly different goal. The intentionality of Fuentes' choice of the *tú* section preceding the Perales episode is underlined by the corresponding *tú* section immediately before the story of Lorenzo's death (pp. 224-8) which is also concerned with the ride of father and son to the river, but now also to the sea, the symbol, as we recognize on p. 226, of a freedom which Artemio, trapped as he is in his materialistic and selfish "order", has irretrievably lost.

The Lorenzo episode itself, perhaps the least convincingly written in the book, because it is the least ambiguous, brings to a climax attended by heroism, love and death, all that Artemio has repressed in himself. Beginning with the dream in the mineshaft in 1915 of a life spent on the land—the reconstructed *hacienda* of Cocuya, Artemio's birthplace, is semi-symbolically handed over to Lorenzo to manage—it ends with Lorenzo's determination to make the moral choice from which his mother has attempted to isolate him and which his father had not dared to ask of him. As Lorenzo embraces what Artemio calls "mi otro destino" (p. 242), the tally of those who die in the latter's place is made up.

In contrast—for, as we have seen continuously, contrast, expressive of Artemio's duality, (and hence that of Mexico, "esta comunidad jánica, de rostro doble", p. 151) is the fundamental technique here—the New Year party episode of 1955 brings to a parallel climax all that Artemio has surrendered to in his life. It is splendidly introduced, and its climactic function clearly underlined, by the *tú* section which precedes it. In that section the authorial commentary which lies concealed in the other *tú* sections breaks surface in order to recapitulate all Artemio's previous wrong choices, the choices which have led up to the moment in 1955 when the cycle of his external success is complete. The conspicuous waste, the parade of material wealth and possessions, the exhibition of power combined with inner frustration and fear, repeat with added emphasis the formula of the "typical day" episode of 1941. The circle of cause and effect, to which the novel so far has been devoted, is closed. The physical presence of Lilia, the allusions to Catalina and Laura, the dialogue with Ceballos in which Lorenzo is always psychologically present, create a pattern of back-references which reinforce the function of the New Year party episode, that of setting the scene for the "resurrección fermentada de todos los hechos . . . palabras y cosas muertas del ciclo" (p. 259): the ancient Mexican fifty-two-year cycle which links 1955 with 1903 and hence the body of the novel with the concluding sequence.

So far, then, the 1919, 1913, 1924 and 1927 episodes can be seen as forming an initial, carefully-organised narrative sequence causally related to the "typical day" of 1941 which corresponds to the conventional exposition. The 1947, 1915 and 1934 episodes, equally deliberately arranged so that the first and last form a frame for the central one, constitute the book's "strong centre", while the 1939 and 1955 episodes, in stark contrast to one another, bring the novel to a clashing climax in which the ultimate betrayal by Artemio of his true destiny and its reward in terms of wealth and power are brutally juxtaposed.

The symbolic fifty-two-year gap separating the 1955 episode from the 1903 episode marks the most audacious articulation in the narrative arrangement as a whole. This is not a smooth transition, but the most heavily-emphasised contrast of all. For it is a double contrast, not only with the beginning of the book, the tycoon day which displaced the 1903 episode as the book's natural exposition, but also with the peak of power, arrogance (and fear): the New Year party. At this point, the beginning of the conclusion, we return to Cocuya, Artemio's birthplace, the "otra tierra" with its *perfume* of innocence and idealism which had stimulated Artemio's daydream in the mine-shaft and had been his natural gift to Lorenzo, their representative. The 1903 episode itself is in two parts: the story of Lunero, Artemio and the *enganchador*, and the story of the Menchacas which is encapsulated within it, the two being linked together by the death of don Pedro. Each part has its role to play in regard to the rest of the novel; together they combine the functions of providing the story's dramatic concluding effect and of constituting at the same time a final ironic commentary on its basic themes. In this way what could have been an anti-climax, the account of Artemio's childhood coming after all we know of him as a man, is transformed into a striking finale.

The Artemio-Lunero-*enganchador* incident is the most difficult part of the novel to relate to the rest of its narrative organisation. In one sense it is profoundly positive, an act of disinterested courage by a boy hardly big enough to hold the weapon with which he commits it. Artemio's intention is to protect Lunero. In addition his action contains an element of poetic justice: Artemio revenges his father's death on the coward who had fled in 1889 instead of fighting. To this extent it symbolises the uncorrupted youth and idealism of Artemio in Cocuya, the heritage of which—resistance to oppression—passes to Lorenzo. But the act is fundamentally ambiguous. Instead of killing the *enganchador*, Artemio unwittingly kills his uncle. In this sense, however well-intentioned, his action is chronologically the first of the "wrong choices" which he makes throughout the rest of the novel. In addition he is symbolically killing a part of himself: that part of the Menchacas, represented by don Pedro, which is soft, passive, lacking in willpower and self-assertion. The killing of don Pedro is the first revelation of the aggressive, cruel and violent side of Artemio's nature, inherited from his father Atanasio, the exploiter and oppressor.

Perhaps the clue to the meaning of the episode is to be sought in the *tú* section immediately preceding the 1919 Puebla episode, one of the basic passages in the novel. More than once in *La muerte de Artemio Cruz*, Artemio appears to be in possession of a "secret". But close scrutiny of the text does not reveal what it is. In fact, there appear to be two secrets, as befits the duality of Artemio himself. One is the moral imperative, accepted by Gonzalo Bernal and Lorenzo, amongst others, to "darlo todo a cambio de nada". The other is enunciated in the *tú* section just referred to: that one can always find "en lo negro el germen, el reflejo de su opuesto" (p. 33), a doctrine of total moral ambiguity. It is surely this doctrine which triumphs in the death of don Pedro, in which good and evil are irretrievably mixed. Despite sundry indications to the contrary contained in the novel, there is good reason to believe that Fuentes is strongly drawn to this outlook.

The story of the Menchacas, the other half of the last big episode, which separates the two parts of the Artemio-Lunero-*enganchador* story, is easier to relate to the general scheme of the novel. It symbolizes the destiny of post-colonial Mexico—significantly, doña Liduvinia was born in 1810—and, as don Gamaliel reflects, "cada generación tiene que destruir a los antiguos poseedores y sustituirlos por nuevos amos, tan rapaces y ambiciosos como los anteriores" (p. 50). As the Menchacas had dispossessed the Indians, so they in turn had been dispossessed under the *Porfiriato*, whose new land-owning class was to be dispossessed by the victors of the Revolution, including Artemio. This circular destiny, which already threatens Artemio on his death-bed, as his grand-daughter entertains her boy-friend in the next room, adds its ambiguity to that of the death of don Pedro. For if all is merely circular, in spite of Juárez, in spite of Madero, what is the meaning of Gonzalo and Lorenzo's sacrifice?

The absence of a clear moral principle and the absence of a clear sense of politico-social progress combine at the end of *La muerte de Artemio Cruz* to modify the implications which we have taken for granted as we absorbed the social criticism which governed so much of the earlier presentation of Artemio and his surroundings. The rather confusing pseudo-philosophic reflections which Fuentes introduces into the penultimate *tú* sequence seem to reinforce the sense of futility which hangs over the end of the novel. For in them Artemio's life is reduced to a trivial incident in a process of cosmic entropy. The secret which he is to discover at the moment of his death seems to be that all is one and the same, all is in all; good and bad, freedom and oppression, all is merely part of the same meaningless downward spiral: "una danza de locura en la que el tiempo devorará al tiempo" (p. 313), a "river of change" (as the same paragraph calls it) without progress or finality. Thus, the conclusion of the book, in which birth and death are juxtaposed, not only modifies retrospectively the picture we have built up of Artemio's life and the modern history of Mexico, but also attempts to set both in a timeless perspective. The struggle—and embrace—of good and evil, which is deeply rooted inside Artemio and inside the historical process of his country is seen to be universal and eternal. In this sense, the ending rounds off the formal design of the novel with a conjunction of events which, like the others we have examined, is both striking in itself and at the same time a meaningful comment on the theme.

In conclusion: the narrative organisation of *La muerte de Artemio Cruz*, far from being an arbitrary jumble, or merely bodying forth a mechanical relationship between private abjection and public success, represents the triumph of a conscious artistic intention over a conventional arrangement of episodes. The ordering of the incidents can be seen on analysis to form a subtly articulated sequence of contrasts and transitions, each of which stands the test of fictional effectiveness. Like the best of the *nuevas novelas*, *La muerte de Artemio Cruz* uses a meticulous fashioning and patterning of the narration to create a fundamentally ambiguous view of reality.

DONALD L. SHAW

Edinburgh

NOTES

[1] See for example R. M. Reeve, "An Annotated Bibliography of Carlos Fuentes, 1949-69", *Hispania*, LIII (1970), 595-652; also in H. F. Giacoman, *Homenaje a Carlos Fuentes*, New York, 1971.

[2] *Nueva narrativa hispanoamericana*, Adelphi University, New York, I, No. 2 (1971), 105-16; also in Giacoman and in Loveluck's *Novelistas hispanoamericanos de hoy*, Madrid, 1976.

[3] "Acotaciones a *La muerte de Artemio Cruz*", in *Coloquio sobre la novela hispano-americana* by I. A. Schulman, M. P. González, J. Loveluck and F. Alegría, Mexico City, 1967, 89-100. Osorio quotes similar reactions from the Chilean critics *Alone* and Cedomil Goic. See too Sommers' reference to the "hopscotch order" in which Artemio's experiences are described (*After the Storm*, p. 156).

[4] See the interview quoted by M. Benedetti in *Letras del continente mestizo*, Montevideo, 1967, p. 164.

[5] All quotations are taken from the third edition, Fondo de Cultura Económica, Mexico City, 1967.

[6] Rodolfo Usigli, *El gesticulador*, Act I, Scene ii. *Obras completas*, Mexico City, 1963, p. 735.

IV

GARCÍA MÁRQUEZ AND THE SECRETS OF
SATURNO SANTOS

General Saturno Santos cannot be numbered among the most salient named "characters" of *El otoño del patriarca*. Yet he has qualities which distinguish him from the others and enlist him among the more powerful hidden forces in the novel. First and foremost, the general is a full-blooded Indian. Of those who once helped the patriarch to power he is the least tractable, the one hardest to elicit from his "lair", and yet so proud as to disdain escort. And of "los últimos herederos de nuestra guerra", the much-reduced band invited to the anniversary celebrations in the presidential palace, he is the only one canny enough to survive, to save himself from the massacre planned by their leader. This capacity for self-preservation is directly attributed to his mysterious Indian knowledge, to secrets which allow him to metamorphose (into armadillo, pond, thunder) and even to revenge himself in his way. He is thus the most sharply-defined example of Indian presence in the novel as a whole. He embodies the barefoot, machete-swinging Guajiro who lends yeoman yet inscrutable service to the patriarch early in that man's career; he carries with him the most pungent and the most tender Indian-village odours, remembered with such deep nostalgia by the patriarch ("la patria entera con su dragón, madre", p. 230); and he cannot be denied a share in the native American voice which re-tells, with amusement and contempt, how Columbus behaved on reaching America (pp. 44-6).

What might be called the Indian engagement in *El otoño* has plenty of antecedents in García Márquez's writings, notably in *Cien años de soledad*. Just as the patriarch, with his household, national geography and climates, may be illuminatingly compared with José Arcadio Buendía, the "patriarch" of Macondo, so Saturno Santos has his kin in the earlier novel. This particular element in García Márquez's writing, unobtrusive as it may rightly seem, deserves attention if nothing else because of the tight-lipped treatment received by Indians in Colombian literature. Unlike the countries to either side, in Mesoamerica and in the Andean republics, Colombia has remained almost silent, literarily, about her Indian populations, even though many of them, Chibcha, Carib and Arawak, are still very much alive; and despite the fact that, as Piedrahita was the first to demonstrate (1688), Colombian history makes sense only when the Indians are taken into account, with their trade routes, calendars, shaman societies and work in gold and stone. As the poet of La Gran Colombia, Andrés Bello, went so far as to make Cundinamarca the focal point of his "America" and to find in the Chibcha doctrine of Bochica echoes of the "world-age" cosmogony shared by the Incas and by the Mesoamericans. Yet before García Márquez, with his investment in the lost heart of Latin America situated between "Riobamba and Veracruz", that El Dorado or third marquisate of America so desired by the Pizarros and by Walter Raleigh[1] alike, we search in vain for any furthering of those insights, apart from a few allusions in Isaacs and in Gutiérrez González's humanly unspecific "Memoria sobre el cultivo del maíz" (1861).

The Indians appearing in *Cien años de soledad* are mainly confined to chapter three, that is, to the stage of the novel when García Márquez is most concerned with origins and beginnings. Though at first only a ghostly presence as fishermen in the swamps around Macondo, where the memory of Tairona warriors and gold-workers is submerged beneath Castilian relics —armour and galleon—, before long they actually enter the Buendía household. Cataure and his sister are presented as royalty from a "millennial kingdom", about which we can only speculate, beyond the fact that the errant pair are said to be Guajiro Indians, Arawak-speakers from the peninsula where Riohacha is to be found, renowned then as now for its vigorous trading spirit.

But this *location* in itself amounts to a great deal. For as the "royal pair", the Guajiro Cataure and his sister are spared the extreme displacement suffered by their counterparts in the Colombian novel published exactly one hundred years before *Cien años*: Isaacs' *María*. Isaacs' African princess Nay and her lover are both more "noble", because of their conveniently remote territorial origin and more patronized, as Colombian slaves. As for the Indians of Colombia, dispossessed of their "millennial kingdom" by slave owners like Isaacs' own father, they are absent from *María*. In fact Indian history is acknowledged by Isaacs only in his "scientific" works, in which he speculated for example on the links between Mexican scripts and the hieroglyphs used by the Guajiro and their neighbours.[2] (Exactly this displacement of *literary* attention from Indian to black, "Macondo to Congo", is found in the writer who most influenced *María*: Chateaubriand. Having set out to vindicate American Indians as "mankind's last chance" in *Les Natchez*, Chateaubriand ended up disrespecting his Indians' very speech, putting into their mouths songs translated by Parny from Malagasy).[3] By allowing his Indian pair to have both a local origin and a millennial history, García Márquez corrects at least this precedent of bad faith.

Together with Rebeca, who arriving soon after Cataure trails her bag of parental bones, eats earth and utters "illegible hieroglyphs", the Indians soon have their effect on the Buendía household, as they pad around with "their stealthy feet". The children learn Arawak before Castilian: their preferring the language of the native "guests" to that of their parents unavoidably affects the balance between the two parties. As if to compensate, José Arcadio takes to overhauling the household's time-keeping system, installing musical clocks of Old World manufacture. These replace the native birds which since the foundation had obligingly "gladdened the passage of time with their fluting"; in fact birds, numbered in series, played a crucial role in the formation of native calendars in Colombia as in Mesoamerica. Growing ever more attached to the Indians and sharing their tastes in food, the children come consciously to defend their decision not to speak Spanish. However, what promises to become an irresolvable conflict is simply removed from the narrative, by the plague of insomnia and amnesia which descends on the household. So much is forgotten that even everyday objects have to be labelled, to be made recognizable. Apart from giving García Márquez the chance to satirize Carpentier's claim that the Latin American writer's duty is to "name the things" of his continent, like another Adam, this plague of amnesia directly anticipates the forgetfulness which, later on, completely erases from everyone's memory the massacre of the banana workers in the interests of U.S. capital. The implication will be clear enough: amnesia is the best aid to understanding the relations of native Americans with *their* continental guests, and necessary for fond dreams that Indian and white were once a happy family.

Neat enough in narrative terms, García Márquez's amnesic event has another side to it, which is harder to interpret. For it is the Indians themselves who carry the plague: Cataure arrives in Macondo from his "reino milenario" in an effort to escape it. What its ultimate source may be, Indian or white, is left unsaid. José Arcadio mockingly suggests that it was "una de tantas dolencias inventadas por la superstición de los indígenas". But despite their historical association with the plague, the Indians are by no means held unequivocally responsible for the "idiotez sin pasado" into which the family is plunged by its insomnia and amnesia. In any case, in *Cien años* this dilemma is left to cancel itself, as part of a discussion which is superseded when "Gabriel Márquez" intervenes directly to help Aureliano to transcend Macondo, and when the narrative "opens" to present the reader with the final cry, which can only demand its contradiction: "because races condemned to one hundred years of solitude did not have a second opportunity on earth" ("porque las estirpes condenadas a cien años de soledad no tenían una segunda oportunidad sobre la tierra").

In *El otoño* no such notional exit exists. The reader is held within the patriarch's "nightmare realm" right to the end. Correspondingly, the Indian presence in this later novel is less episodic, and less passive. While Cataure merely pads through the Buendía house, the barefoot Guajiro in *El otoño* literally slashes out a trail for the President, his machete being the first instrument to national power. With it, the same Indian also slices up the wronged husband Poncio Daza with fiendish expertise; he displays the same mixture of skill and bewitchment as Saturno Santos does before being "pardoned" and adopted as the patriarch's intimate and *compadre* (228). Indeed, behaviour of this kind lends credence to the likely Indian origin of the "curses" dreamt and feared by the insomniac patriarch himself, when contemplating the deaths of his mother and of his child by Leticia. This last combines the horror of the piranha and ant scenes in *La vorágine*[4] with the pathos of the dead child in *Cien años* (and hence Cortázar's *Rayuela*). As for the mother, her rotting body, stained red, yellow and blue by medicaments, is the only phenomenon to survive the plague which afflicts her son: an amnesia far more hallucinatory than that suffered by the Buendías.

Unlike Cataure (who leaves the moment amnesia arrives), Saturno Santos cannot in any way be disentangled from his patriarch; he is unequivocally party to the plague of the realm. With his Indian humour, Saturno Santos is the one man the patriarch can rely on to share a good cowboy joke ("astucia de vaqueros"). And the complicity between them may of itself be seen to explain much of their nation's disastrous history. This point is made quite obvious in the figure of the *Indian* Rubén Darío, who bemuses the patriarch further, as if out of some immensely elaborate revenge, distracting him from the sordid helplessness of his realm with "the revelation of written beauty").

The mention of Darío has to lead us back to Asturias's portrait of the dictator Estrada Cabrera whose honoured guest the Nicaraguan poet was, and whose habits are alluded to elsewhere in *El otoño*, in the lampshades of human skin, for example; and in the patriarch's fascination with comets and his desire to be acknowledged "corrector of earthquakes, eclipses and leap-years", like the latter-day Maya shaman-priest Estrada Cabrera aspired to be. The parallel is important since for Asturias the realm of *El señor presidente* and the magic jungle of the Maya *Hombres de maíz* are in the last analysis identical. Both lie beyond the pale of bourgeois rationalism and liberal tolerance. For all his interest in the Maya, especially their classic literature, Asturias never quite made good the racism of his first book,[5] nor the fact that his first model for the President was the Quiche-Maya rain god Tohil, whose fearsome cult is described at length in the *Popol vuh*.

Close as García Márquez is to Asturias in the suggestion of this Indian complicity, he does not stop short as his predecessor does. Rather he follows it through, not separating the Indians off morally and geographically as something alien to himself, the authorial presence. And he goes to new lengths in his enquiries into time, a dimension of *El otoño* which cannot ultimately be divorced from its Indian elements. Formally strengthening devices used in *Cien años*, he accounts the movements of time not at all in years A.D. or "of our era" but in rounds of weekdays and months. In the tropical latitudes of the patriarch's realm, the months lose all their traditional associations, except perhaps as indicators of altitude: the ill-fated children of the lottery shift "from Novembers to Februaries" when transported from the coast to the highlands. The months certainly have no seasonal identity, which lends irreality to the novel's title in all but an entirely individual sense ("*su otoño*"). These rounds of weekdays and months—October Friday, April Tuesday—acquire exactly the kind of self-validating, cyclic fatedness which characterizes the signs used in native American ritual and calendrics. Acts and events are identified, even defined by these temporal signs, which serve as a main means of connection and coherence, as when we pass on page 183 from one Wednesday to "another Wednesday of another era of the nation".

A term which García Márquez makes appropriate to this other valency of time is "prehistoric", used to describe the floods of a past world age and the riverine lairs from which "dragons" threaten in *El otoño*, and applied in *Cien años* to the egg-like stones in Macondo's clear river and the hunger of the ants who devour the last scion of the Buendías. Like Macondo, the patriarch's realm is impinged on periodically from the outside but lacks a *linear* time of its own. And it is just this difference which tests most severely the linearity so insisted upon in Western chronology, be it in liberal nationalism or in Marxist notions of historical process. One of the more intricate conflicts resulting from the Old World invasion of the New has been chronological; for the most enduring bonds of García Márquez's native Colombia with the Quechua and the Mesoamericans has been through calendrical philosophy, in which units of time (e.g. days as against years) and their serial beginnings and endings find their own geopolitical reason.[6] García Márquez's double-edged handling of chronology in *El otoño* culminates in the startling final phrases of the novel, which bring the "good news" that with the Patriarch's death "el tiempo incontable de la eternidad había por fin terminado".

To make any sense of this paradox we have to assess what is happening altogether in the last page and a half of the novel, which like the ending of *Cien años* stands in an odd relationship with all the preceding narrative. Leading up to these final phrases, with the patriarch's definitive death García Márquez adopts the first person plural, speaking as one with the poor and oppressed who, loving with an "insatiable passion" and knowing "who we were", can look forward to a better future. The only thing which prevents this from amounting to outright sarcasm—a cry of despair where the ending of *Cien años* had been the provocation of hope—is the use made of this first person plural earlier in the novel. The speakers in these previous cases are also the oppressed, usually anonymous though sometimes identifiable, for example as the whores decked out as schoolgirls obliged to indulge the weirder sexual tastes of the patriarch in his senility. But by far the most sustained of these "we" passages is the one which concludes the first section (44-6). There, García Márquez makes his bold leap into the consciousness of the Carib-"cannibals" who welcomed Columbus. Daring taboos, which "indigenism" of itself has not removed, the narrative incorporates the Indian voice as the first "we", the point of reference in time and in incredulous irony for what subsequent solidarity there is to be found in the book.

Within the range of meanings to be read in this exasperated and inexhaustible novel, all this is tantamount to saying that upon the "secrets" proper to Saturn Santos, the Guajiros and their kin, are predicated modes of survival, behaviour and attitudes whose force cannot be simply suppressed or dismissed as "Indian" and therefore alien. And with that belong two further propositions whose contradiction the novel does nothing to resolve yet which proves more apparent than real: that Latin America's patriarchs owe their most intimate support to their victims of longest standing; and that (as Artaud argued)[7] America's revolution is inconceivable without the Indian.

GORDON BROTHERSTON

Essex

NOTES

[1] According to his *The discoverie of the large, rich and bewtiful land of Guiana*, London, 1596 (which is remarkable for a closeness to the Indians typified by the author's preparedness to smoke tobacco). See also Lucas Fernández de Piedrahita, *Noticia historial de las conquistas del Nuevo Reino de Granada* (1688), Bogotá, 1973, 2 vols.; Bello's source for the Bochica legend was A. von Humboldt's *Vue des cordillères*, Paris, 1816. It is worth noting that the historian who popularized pre-Columbian Mexico and Peru in English, W. H. Prescott, all but wrote a third volume on the territory between; see his letter to Acosta printed in H. R. Lemly, "Who was El Dorado?", *Century Magazine*, October 1891, p. 892.

[2] In his *Estudio sobre las tribus indígenas del estado de Magdalena* (1884), Bogotá, 1951.

[3] See G. Chinard's magisterial edition of *Les Natchez*, Paris, 1932.

[4] Much in Rivera's novel may in turn be derived from the lore of Amazonia and Indian America generally, beyond the salient example of the Mapiripana episode; see for example the Witoto texts studied by K. T. Preuss. (Preuss was also responsible for initiating Colombian archeology, at San Agustín, in 1913.)

[5] *El problema social del indio* (1923), ed. C. Couffon, Paris, 1971; on this generally see my *The Emergence of the Latin American Novel*, Cambridge, 1977, which also has fuller references to Carpentier and to *Cien años*.

[6] On the American system of world ages and the ritual bases of its Indian calendars see my *Image of the New World: a Continent Portrayed through Native American Texts*, London, 1979.

[7] He discusses the prospects of what he calls "la révolution indienne" in articles on Mexico collected in Volumes VIII and IX of his *Œuvres Complètes*, Paris, 1971. A rather different assessment of the first person plural used in *El otoño* is made by Julio Ortega in his comprehensive article, "*El otoño del patriarca*: texto y cultura", *Eco*, XXXIII (1978), 678-99, though among the "teatro de voces" in the novel, he does define it as "un 'nosotros' que deduce el mayor espesor informativo".

V

ONETTI AND THE MEANING OF FICTION:
NOTES ON *LA MUERTE Y LA NIÑA*

Facts, Onetti has said, "son siempre vacíos, son recipientes que tomarán la forma del sentimiento que los llene".[1] Another way of putting this would be to say that facts are relative—doubly so, if they are already part of a fiction—and that their links with the idea of a stable "reality" are more tenuous than might seem. Or one might go further and claim, as many recent novelists have done, that there is no clear and final division between the real and the fictive, and that any kind of language which appears to deny this is by definition false.[2]

At one point in Onetti's most recent novel, *La muerte y la niña* (1973), the question of the possible relation between fact and fiction is raised in a peculiarly direct form:

> No importa qué recetó el médico para el resfrío de Augusto Goerdel, que tenía once años de edad en el tiempo de la coincidencia supuesta. Esto puede rastrearse, si importara, en los libros de Barthé, boticario, concejal y nuevamente boticario. Lo que importa es ignorar para siempre—y aquí hay una especie de felicidad—qué conversó, qué supo, qué dedujo el Padre Bergner en la posible visita que, se nos antoja, fue crepuscular, lenta y tranquila (32).[3]

The "reality" to which this refers is clearly an intrinsic part of the story: the contrast is between the unimportance of facts which can be checked (the doctor's visit, which actually took place) and the importance of what can only remain a speculation (the "possible" visit of the priest and his imagined encounter with the doctor). And the latter is important precisely because it leaves the imagination free to create its own vision of events; fact, in other words, has had to give way to fiction, and it is in this moving away from facts—or, alternatively, in the way facts themselves are deformed by being incorporated in the fiction—that the possibility of a story may take shape.

The opening situation of *La muerte y la niña* presents certain facts which in themselves form the elements of a plot: A tells B that his (A's) wife will die if she conceives a second child; she eventually does this and dies as predicted. Stated in this way, the plot has only limited possibilities: a prediction is fulfilled in such a way that there is neither surprise nor suspense. Yet, though there is more to the opening chapters than this suggests, the bare facts are not without their own narrative implications. In the first place, as Fredric Jameson reminds us, prediction and prophecy are closely related to the act of speech: "Prophecy . . ., insofar as it redoubles everything that will actually happen, . . . causes us to see in events, not their existential immediacy, but a mere confirmation of speech itself, as events-already-narrated".[4] Secondly, the appearance of A represents an intrusion into the life of B, the introduction of a foreign element which will perhaps call for readjustments on the part of B, and which in turn may prolong the story beyond the point at which the initial plot—the prediction and its fulfilment —is completed.

To give the characters concerned their actual names, it is this unexpected intrusion of Augusto Goerdel into the life of the doctor, Díaz Grey, which generates the story that follows. The visit itself, clearly, is paradoxical: the "patient" is not ill and the doctor is unable to write him a prescription.[5] Though the fact of the prediction emphasizes Goerdel's rôle as a storyteller, the first chapter of the novel opens just after his confession has ended, and it is through the reflections of Díaz Grey that the reader is made aware of what has taken place. For the latter, Goerdel is a future murderer who will commit a "crime", though one which is not legally punishable. This already involves recasting what I have called the "initial plot": Goerdel is now a man who announces in advance that he will perform a murder. There is apparently no doubt as to the nature of the "crime", the victim, the time or the manner, nor, for that matter, about the impossibility of retribution. Thus a gap is immediately created between what Díaz Grey is being told and his intuitive reading of Goerdel's information: it is he himself who introduces the language of murder and criminal investigation, and who senses that he and others, by hearing Goerdel's confession, are being made to act like witnesses in a court case.[6] Goerdel, for his part, presents the situation merely as a dilemma, ultimately insoluble because of his religious convictions, but which he has already taken steps to postpone by arranging to absent himself for a time from his wife.

What generates the story, therefore, is not the prediction itself, but the question "Why is he telling me this?"[7] In the course of the first chapter, the various attempts at an explanation founder against a basic impenetrability. Goerdel, in recounting his situation, is fabricating a "plot"—in both senses of the word—which has its aesthetic dimension (he is perfecting a "crime" which is not a crime) (10); in his reading of Goerdel, Díaz Grey detects "la trampa, la hipocresía, la congénita astucia" (all qualities which are emphasized in the account of Goerdel's upbringing in Chapters III and IV) (11). Similarly, Goerdel's own explanation of his visit—"El conflicto, repito, sólo es mío. Por eso le pedí esta entrevista."—not only confirms Díaz Grey's suspicions but increases his sense of frustration: "No sólo por eso, hijo de perra; hay un espanto detrás, hay un cálculo. Se sentía más débil que su visitante, empezaba a odiarlo con franqueza" (13).[8] And his final reaction is to feel trapped by something he cannot put into words: "acorralado . . . por una trampa, una sutileza mayor, un presentimiento indefinible, grumoso y repelente" (17).

Thus the possibility of a story arises from the notion of an enigma to be resolved. As Josefina Ludmer has pointed out, there is a real sense in which Díaz Grey narrates precisely because he is in a state of ignorance:

". . . en Onetti el médico es el que no sabe y narra *porque* no sabe: el relato
es búsqueda e investigación; el médico no cura, no 'practica' la medicina en
los relatos; no es visitador . . . sino visitado: se sitúa en su espacio y recibe
relatos".[9] The spatial reference in the last phrase also suggests another
means by which Onetti's fictions are produced: the fact that so many of
the characters are situated between pairs of opposites which, by formalizing
the element of difference, create a field of tensions within which the narrative
must attempt to find its balance.[10] So, in *La muerte y la niña*, Augusto
Goerdel exists between several sets of poles: Santa María and the Colonia
Suiza, doctor and priest, one child and another, the religious life and the
secular, and, later, between the Old World and the New. Díaz Grey, for his
part, speaks of his long-absent daughter in a voice which is *between* the past
and the present (75), and at another point uses similar terms to refer to his
own "birth" as a fictional character: "una de las formas de su condena
incomprensible [i.e. his creator's] era haberme traído al mundo en una edad
invariable *entre* la ambición con tiempo limitado y la desesperanza" (56.
Italics mine).

The "creator" in this last instance is Brausen, the mention of whom
brings into play the whole question of Díaz Grey's status as a fictional
character. In *La vida breve* (1950), the novel which initiates the Santa María
sequence, Juan María Brausen is himself a fictional character who invents
a sub-fiction based on the imaginary town of Santa María, in which the
chief protagonist is Díaz Grey.[11] By the end of that novel, as the result of
a complex process of overlapping identities, Díaz Grey has achieved the
status of independent narrator, and Brausen has disappeared as a person,
to become the mythical "fundador" whose statue stands in the square of
Santa María, and later the "Dios-Brausen" of *La muerte y la niña* and other
stories. What this means is that, from the end of *La vida breve* onwards,
Díaz Grey is both a writer (in contrast to other characters who are non-
writers or simple informants)[12] and a character who is aware that he is a
fictional creation.

One result of this is that Díaz Grey has only as much reality as Brausen
allows him, a phenomenon which contributes to the fragmentation which is
taken to greater lengths in *La muerte y la niña* than in any of Onetti's previous fiction. This assumes various forms: in the first place, the text refers
several times to Díaz Grey's childhood and student days, that is to say, to
a part of his life which antedates his first appearance as a fictional character
in *La vida breve*.[13] Yet what is striking is not so much that Díaz Grey has
been provided with a past of which there was no mention in the earlier
stories,[14] but that his memories of this past should lack any sense of continuity. Secondly, this inability to relate memories to one another is shared,
on a smaller scale, by Jorge Malabia, though the subject here is the doctor
himself: "Malabia se detuvo y comenzó a mirarlo como recordando, como
si pudiera aislar dentro de los años, cada vez que había visto al médico. Y

estos recuerdos se mantenían independientes, unidos apenas por el nombre"
(71). And, significantly, it is Malabia who, a moment later, invites Díaz
Grey to explain his past: "Pero, y sí me interesa, conocer su pasado, saber
quién, qué era usted, doctor, antes de mezclarse con los habitantes de Santa
María. Los fantasmas que inventó e impuso Juan María Brausen" (71-72).
It is Malabia's question which leads Díaz Grey to speak for the first time of
the daughter, now an adolescent, whom he has not seen since she was three
years old. The years of his daughter's infancy represent "el otro mundo
perdido" (80); in the intervening time, someone (the mother who is never
named?) has continued to send him photographs of her: "otros retratos,
otras caras que iban trepando bruscamente las edades, no se sabía hacia
dónde, pero sí alejándose de lo que yo había visto y querido, de lo que me
era posible recordar. Con permiso de Brausen, naturalmente" (77). This
last phrase, with its evident irony, reinforces the sense that, here and elsewhere, the character in question has unexpectedly been provided with a
fragmentary past for the sake of this particular story—more specifically,
that it is important for the present narrative that Díaz Grey himself should
be a father.

Finally, there are the two events which must come as a surprise to
readers who know the earlier stories in the sequence: Díaz Grey's marriage
to Angélica Inés Petrus, whose insanity is described in *El astillero*, and the
reappearance of Padre Bergner, the mentor of Augusto Goerdel, whose death
is recorded in the same novel. Clearly, there is nothing inherently impossible
in the fact of the marriage, however unlikely it might seem; what is significant,
however, is the lack of any explanation as to how it came about. Given the
complete absence of motivation, there is nothing on which the reader could
speculate, so that again one is left with the sense that it is the needs of the
story itself which have generated a particular situation, as if it were essential
to the whole for Díaz Grey to be not only a father but a husband, although
this dual rôle demands the existence of two separate women.[15] The reappearance of Bergner, however, is another matter: in one way, it is a
deliberate flouting of "realism"; in another, it is as if Onetti had responded
with ironic literalness to the words uttered by Díaz Grey in his final conversation with the priest: "Concedido, padre. Tampoco (Brausen) se equivocó
con usted. Santa María lo necesita. Casi diría que esta ciudad no es conce-
bible sin usted, ni usted sin la ciudad" (100). Yet, in a more profound sense,
Bergner's presence is necessary since he represents another variation on the
theme of paternity which lies at the centre of the book.[16] Not only is he
Goerdel's "spiritual father", as he himself asserts at a crucial point in the
same interview (97); Goerdel, humanly speaking, is to a great extent his own
creation—a relationship which is deeply embedded in the communal history
of Santa María and the Colonia, and which, for the purposes of the story,
must be prolonged as completely as possible into the present.[17]

One effect of such fragmentation is to dispel the illusion that what we are reading is in some way a transcript of "real events" and to confirm our sense of a text which is being created in accordance with its own internal laws. This is a point I shall return to later; in the meantime, it is important to recognize how this process is compounded by the ambiguous status of Brausen himself. Thus, if by this stage Brausen is the "god" of Santa María, it is significant that at one point he is referred to as a "demiurge", that is to say, as the creator of a world who at the same time is subordinate to a supreme god: "Está obligado, por respeto a las grandes tradiciones que desea imitar, a irme matando, célula a célula, síntoma a síntoma. Pero también tiene que seguir el monótono ejemplo de los innumerables demiurgos anteriores y ordenar vida y reproducción" (24). Here it is Díaz Grey who is reflecting ironically on the fact that his life is permanently out of phase with that of the girls he sees around him. And a moment later, he turns on the "creator" who is responsible for this:

> Ellas siempre lejanas e intocables, apartadas de mí por la disparidad de los treinta o cuarenta años que me impuso Juan María Brausen, maldita sea su alma que ojalá se abrase durante uno o dos pares de eternidades en el infierno adecuado que ya tiene pronto para él un Brausen más alto, un poco más verdadero (25).

The situation recalls that of Borges's story *Las ruinas circulares*, another parable of fictional creation. Here, the notion of a superior god is surely a reference to the novelist himself, whose hidden hand controls the apparently self-sufficient Brausen. Yet the chain of hierarchy this suggests is less simple than it looks, since *La muerte y la niña*, like Onetti's other fictions, seems to imply that the potential writer can only become an "author" when his material—the nucleus of the story—supplies the conditions necessary for the construction of the text to go forward. Whatever the truth of this, the peculiar distinction of *La muerte y la niña* is that it presents a god in decline, a fact which is reflected in the situation of Santa María itself.

Throughout the novel, Brausen is described as inscrutable, tyrannical and indifferent; the striking thing, however, is that these qualities are related to the action of time. The change this implies is symbolized by the equestrian statue of Brausen which commemorates the "founding" of Santa María. This statue, which portrays Brausen with the features of a *caudillo*, has already absorbed him into a national myth. In *La muerte y la niña*, both Bergner and Díaz Grey have the impression that the appearance of the statue is changing: "Y fue el padre Bergner el primero a descubrir, luego de santiguarse, a la luz de los faroles de la plaza, que la cara del jinete de la estatua dedicada a Juan María Brausen, había comenzado a insinuar rasgos vacunos" (49-50). When Bergner looks at the statue by daylight, "la dureza del bronce no mostraba signo alguno de formación de cuernos; sólo una placidez de vaca solitaria y rumiante" (50); nevertheless, the sensation remains, and Bergner's suspicions are later confirmed by Díaz Grey: "Pero el jinete, sí, siempre le sospeché equívocos" (94). A moment later, Díaz Grey recalls the inauguration ceremony described in *El astillero* (*Obras completas*, 1177):

> Pero durante la inauguración y los discursos—siguió el médico—el caballo tiraba a vaca mansa y la figura de arriba tenía rasgos de potro, de bestia indomable. No volví a verlos con atención. Pero deben haber seguido el proceso. La vaca mansa y el jinete bigotudo. Pero no olvide que la vaca da leche pero también sabe cornear (94).

Thus the cow-like features are themselves ambiguous: on the one hand, they suggest passivity, complacency and lack of authority; on the other, the speculation concerning the presence or absence of horns hints at more brutal, and possibly diabolical, associations.[18]

The deterioration of Brausen extends in a curious way to the city itself. By comparison with the earlier stories in the sequence, the topography of Santa María in *La muerte y la niña* is noticeably vague: at one point it is large enough to be the centre of a police state (72), though at another (53) grass is growing beneath Díaz Grey's window in what was once a busy square. At a less literal level, however, these impressions cease to conflict: at the beginning of the book, Díaz Grey refers to "estos restos de Santa María" (10), and towards the end, in his denunciation of all that Santa María stands for, Goerdel can see it both as a "country" with its distinctive national faults and as "lo que persisten en llamar ciudad, y sólo es un poblado del siglo dieciséis" (127). What links the two visions, clearly, is the sense of living in an imaginary creation whose persistence or erosion depend on the vitality or otherwise of its "creator". Just as Brausen, in *La vida breve*, is the narrator who brings into existence an invented world, so his elevation to god-like status and his subsequent deterioration make it possible to conceive the eventual destruction both of himself and of the fictional community for which he is responsible.[19] As usual, it is Díaz Grey who recognizes this possibility, in the course of discussing the statue: "Con perdón de usted, padre, creo que tendremos vida para divertirnos con el terremoto que se lleve al mismísimo infierno al matungo y al jinete ambiguo. Lástima que Santa María esté tan lejos de los Andes" (94).[20]

By drawing attention to its own genesis as a work of fiction, *La muerte y la niña* both defeats the reader's conventional expectations and confronts him with the possibility that the "meaning" of the story may lie not so much in a paraphraseable content as in the actual activity he is compelled to pursue in his attempt to "make sense" of the text. What complicates this process is Onetti's characteristic strategy of taking certain elements associated with more traditional forms of fiction and combining them in untraditional ways.[21] One such form is the detective story, a type of narrative which seems to hold a special fascination for the practitioners of the *Nouveau roman* and which Onetti has more than once reconstructed for his own purposes. The source of this fascination is not far to seek: the detective story, as Stephen Heath has pointed out, "offers a deep confirmation of the non-problematic nature of reality in absenting writing before an ultimate untroubled truth. In this, . . . (it) may be seen as the very type of the 'Balzacian' novel with its premiss of a realist writing that declares itself transparent before the fixed source of 'Reality' ".[22] Detective novels, one could add, involve clear chains of cause and effect; an apparent "mystery" is used to set up a hermeneutical game in the course of which motives are rehearsed and clues interpreted until the investigation ends in a solution and "normality" is restored. Moreover, the reader who seeks for clues pays a particular kind of attention to the text; as John Sturrock remarks: "The general effect of a detective story is to inflate what it contains with potential meaning, and to show how a plot can seize on anything it likes . . . and integrate it within a single meaningful, literary structure".[23]

If one turns back to *La muerte y la niña* with such notions in mind, certain facts emerge which seem to cast a light on the nature of the book as a whole. As we have seen, the opening chapters establish a situation which involves what may or not be a potential crime. The idea of criminality, however, exists only in the mind of Díaz Grey, for whom Goerdel's strategy in announcing his predicament is a means of perfecting a "crime" for which there can be no legal punishment. Thus the subsequent investigation concerns, not a murder, nor even the cause of a death, but the motives which lie behind Goerdel's confession and, later, his wife's parallel visits to Díaz Grey. As in a conventional detective story, the chronology at this point invites the reader to look for clues. Nevertheless, such dates as are given fail to form a consistent pattern: in the opening chapter, the Goerdels' first child is thirteen months old; in the second chapter, which refers to the following day (23), we are told that Helga Goerdel's visits took place "más de un año atrás" (23), and that before seeing Díaz Grey, she had consulted specialists in Europe (21). The impossible coincidence of dates ("trece meses" and "más de un año") seems deliberate, as if defying the reader to construct an accurate chronology—as he would be able to do if the story were obeying the traditional conventions.

If, as Díaz Grey suspects, there are hidden motives behind these visits, he fails to discover them. Once the death of Helga Goerdel occurs, this particular question lapses, to be replaced by Díaz Grey's problematical investigation into his own past. Nevertheless, the question of motive arises again on two different occasions in the later stages of the novel, both times in connection with Goerdel. As a narrator, Goerdel tells three separate, though interdependent, stories in the course of the book: (i) the original prediction; (ii) his dream of the Insauberry girl, and (iii) his account of the letters by which he hopes to establish that he was not the father of the child who caused his wife's death.

The last two stories correspond to the two return visits which Goerdel pays to Santa María. The collective verdict on the first of these is left in no doubt: "(No) pudimos—ni podemos ahora—creer en ninguna respuesta convincente sobre su corta, innecesaria visita. . . El visto bueno de Brausen debió ser motivado por una causa secreta, por un plan que no pudimos comprender hasta que tuvimos nietos. Ni siquiera entender convencidos" (92). The second occasion is more complex: Goerdel has returned a second time to Santa María—he has now remarried and is living in East Germany under an assumed name—in order to make public a series of letters which he claims were written by the true father of Helga's second child. For once, therefore, his motive seems clear, though almost immediately doubts begin to arise. For Jorge Malabia, who is the first to be shown the letters, there is something insane about Goerdel's wish to publish "las que él llama pruebas de una injusticia que a nadie puede doler después de tantos años" (111-112). Díaz Grey, on the other hand, cannot accept the simple explanation of madness: "No debe estar loco, pensé; obstinación, desprecio, una idea fija. El hombre parecía resuelto a cruzar como demente todas las murallas de los cuerdos; a violar, lúcido, todos los obstáculos que construyéramos nosotros, herederos de la locura del bienestar, del invariable ser en la pasividad" (119).

In the interview which follows, Goerdel is a troubling presence who is creating a situation which Díaz Grey finds difficult to interpret: "Nunca pude saber si estaba improvisando el infortunio o si recitaba un discurso sabido de memoria. . . Busqué diagnósticos, síndromes, seguro de no acertar" (120). Later, however, Díaz Grey believes he has detected a secret motive: "Y después comprendí que no había regresado sólo para luchar contra la calumnia y la injusticia. Quería hablar de sí mismo, quería explicarse, quería cubrir con desinteresado cinismo un tiempo de su pasado, la anécdota de una mujer muerta, años atrás, no por él sino por una niña, voluntad insondable de Brausen" (122). Once again, as in the opening chapter, the emphasis is on Goerdel as storyteller; the verb "cubrir" contains a possible ambiguity: he wishes to "cover" a portion of his past by providing himself with an alibi, but there is also the sense in which one tells a story in order to "cover" a void, to postpone the final lapse into silence and death.[24] Yet in the end, Goerdel leaves the letters to speak for themselves, as if the written text were a guarantee of truth. But this is precisely what they fail to do. In the final chapter, Malabia and Díaz Grey scrutinize the letters "con fingidas impaciencias" (132), as if they were consciously parodying the preliminaries to a decisive revelation. Their conclusions are set out in the form of "evidence", but they offer no clear solution: the letters could be genuine or forged (since they are only photocopies, it is impossible to determine their age) and the signature (a capital H) is unidentifiable. Though both Malabia and Díaz Grey seem prepared to doubt the authenticity of the letters, nothing is certain, and Díaz Grey's comment—". . . que los muertos entierren a sus muertos. Y que los hijos de perra se conserven fieles a su destino" (135)—closes the "case" simply by reiterating the opinion of Goerdel expressed on the first page of the novel.

Thus the detective story is emptied of its traditional content by a systematic distortion of its basic constituents. The "crime" is not a crime, the investigation of motives leads nowhere, the possible forgery is never proved and the investigators are indifferent to the attempt to reach a solution. In other words, not only is the pursuit of knowledge finally frustrated, but the whole nature of what there is to know becomes problematical. The parodic element, moreover, not only affects the plot, but also extends to the rôles of the major characters. Where in the realist novel the doctor is traditionally the bearer of knowledge, Díaz Grey gropes his way through a situation he never fully understands and achieves no final illumination. The other confessor-figure, Padre Bergner, is a priest who has no knowledge of souls— "las almas serán siempre desconocidas" (43)—and whose faith in the guidance of Brausen is eventually rewarded with silence. And similarly with the younger characters: Goerdel is a disciple of Bergner, but not in a religious sense, and Malabia's relations with Díaz Grey, though retaining some of the features of mentorship apparent in earlier stories, have reached a state of crisis from which they may or may not emerge intact.

This distortion of conventional rôles, together with the ambiguous allusions to the detective story form, may suggest a mainly negative approach to fiction, designed chiefly to confound the reader's normal expectations. This shock element in itself, clearly, has a positive side insofar as it enforces a closer attention to the text and a more critical attitude towards literary stereotypes. At the same time, there is a much deeper sense in which *La muerte y la niña* hints at the sources of fiction in general, partly through its treatment of the theme of paternity, and partly through its handling of the whole question of sexual relationships. Here again, as I have already suggested, there are ambiguities: Goerdel is a father, though by the end of the novel the paternity of his second child is in doubt; Bergner is a "father", though in a spiritual, not a material, sense, and eventually his hold over Goerdel is broken; Díaz Grey has a daughter, but the identity of the mother is never revealed. It is this last relationship in particular which gives depth to the story—literally so, since it refers to a past which is irrecoverable, but whose memory it is necessary to preserve, since it represents the only kind of love which Díaz Grey has experienced, a permanent source of suffering which has become inseparable from his sense of identity.

The first mention of the daughter occurs, significantly, in the context of sexual love:

> El amor se había ido de la vida de Díaz Grey y a veces, haciendo solitarios o jugando a solas al ajedrez, pensaba confuso si alguna vez lo había tenido de verdad. A pesar de la hija ausente, sólo conocida por malas fotografías, que ahora, fatalmente, estaba bamboleándose en la dichosa sucia adolescencia y cuyo nacimiento no podía prescindir de un prólogo (22).

The use of the word "prólogo" can hardly be casual: her birth must have had a "prologue"—it must have been preceded by some feeling for the mother—but, as far as this particular woman is concerned, no "story" followed. What follows, in effect, is a different kind of story, one made possible by the fact that Díaz Grey is a father. This story, which is essentially that of Díaz Grey's own past and its possible repercussions on the present, could be said to grow out of the absence of the mother—another instance of a narrative which is constructed in order to compensate for a lack. What is even more striking, however, is the sense that it is Díaz Grey himself who has "given birth" to his daughter, rather as, in *La vida breve*, it is the male —Brausen—who "gives birth" to the writing in response to the sexual mutilation of his wife.[25]

Díaz Grey's involvement with his daughter is the subject of Chapter IX, the final part of his conversation with Jorge Malabia. The whole of this chapter is a reply to Malabia's question concerning his past: "Díaz Grey se levantó y trajo hasta el escritorio dos juegos de naipes y un sobre hinchado de fotografías y cartas.—Hay un pasado—dijo casi con asombro, como si no lo entendiera del todo" (75). It is clear from this opening that "daughter" and "past" are synonymous, insofar as the past represents for him a kind of emotional truth, "algo que importaba, sin dudas, más que ella o que yo: mi amor a la niña de tres años" (77). Thus the game with the photographs becomes a "truth game" whose justification lies in the suffering it entails: "Y entonces . . . yo jugaba el gran solitario; miraba las caras atento y calmoso para sufrir mejor, para que el juego valiera la pena . . ." (78-79). One of the characteristics of the "game" is the elimination of chance: even when they are laid face downwards, the identity of the photographs is clear, since their dates are written on the back. Another is that it can never be lost or won: "un juego que siempre moría sin dejarme saber si había ganado o perdido" (78). Thus the "game" is more an exercise in meditation than a true game, unlike the game of patience which it replaces. The contrast could hardly be clearer: as against the arbitrary systems of the patience cards, the photographs represent an unchangeable ritual, more akin to the repeated playing of the "discos sacros" than to the shifting alternatives of chance.[26] Nevertheless, there is a difference: if the photographs never vary, the images they convey remain a constant source of speculation. Those taken in infancy belong to "el otro mundo perdido" (80): it is the three-year-old girl who represents a lost possibility of love; the later ones, on the other hand, though no less "real" as images, are deformations of the original, to compensate for which Díaz Grey constructs a "faceless woman", a blank which his imagination can feed on without fear of contradiction. It is this last desperate attempt to deny "reality" which relates Díaz Grey's action to the process of fictional creation, to the notion, already apparent in much of Onetti's work, that fiction can only arise as the result of a deliberate break with "reality", or, alternatively, that facts matter only to the extent that they provide material for conjecture.

Díaz Grey's own explanation ends in ambiguity:

> Y alguna noche que no será más triste que las otras, quemaré todas las fotos cuya edad pasa los tres años. Si me decidí a pensarla mujer sin cara no fue porque ella se estuviera convirtiendo en una mujer distinta, año tras año, un remiso correo tras el otro. Lo hice porque no tuve fuerzas para tolerar que ella fuese una persona (80).

On the face of it, this might seem to mean that he cannot bear to think of his daughter as a separate individual with a life of her own. But there may well be an echo of something which has been said of him earlier in the novel: "Las mujeres no le importaban de verdad: eran personas" (23)—in other words, they do not interest him as women, they are just "people". On this reading, therefore, he is not prepared to accept that she has become "just another person". The distinction is important, since the second possibility implies a kind of degradation which is not necessarily present in the first. In Onetti's world, to be "degraded"—not in a moral sense, but simply by being "ordinary"—is to cease to be a subject around whom fictions can accumulate.[27] That the Díaz Grey of *La muerte y la niña* can place women in general in this category is perhaps a function of his marginality, the apparently self-appointed rôle from which he can still be shaken by particular circumstances. His composure, certainly, can still be troubled by the presence of an enigma, and the greatest enigma of all concerns his sense of the "otro mundo perdido" symbolized by his three-year-old daughter. It is this sense of "otherness", whether embodied in space or time, which indicates most forcibly the gap between common reality and the unfamiliar, the world of "difference" in which all true fictions are rooted.

Within this world, women occupy a privileged position, both as agents and sufferers. In *La muerte y la niña*, the theme is first suggested at the end of the opening conversation between Goerdel and Díaz Grey. It is possible, says Goerdel, that his wife may have discussed her situation with other people: "Pero no es imposible que ella, tan desesperada como yo, y además mujer, haya hablado con amigas o parientes. Las mujeres, es distinto. Creen, como los enfermos crónicos, usted lo sabe mejor que yo, que si divulgan sus problemas van obteniendo una ayuda, o por lo menos un apoyo, a cambio de cada confidencia" (17). This notion that women inhabit a different world is reinforced in Chapter II, where Díaz Grey reflects on the lover's momentary awareness of the other's mortality: "Aquel momento verdadero en que uno de los amantes, casi nunca la mujer porque se sabe, y es cierto, inmortal, celosamente repetida desde el principio y hacia el infinito" (24). Woman as representative of the irrational, the cyclical and the continuous: these are familiar themes, in literature as elsewhere. Yet in *La muerte y la niña*, as in other stories by Onetti ("La cara de la desgracia", *Para una tumba sin nombre*), the narrative hinges on the death of a woman, the event without which this particular story could not exist. In terms of Onetti's fictional strategy, this suggests two things: that women represent a world of "difference" in relation to which a male character is able to assume his rôle as narrator, and that, in a profoundly unrealistic sense, women die in his fictions because they are unable to tell stories themselves. The first proposition is easier to grasp than the second, though the two are ultimately inseparable. In its most extreme form, its field of operation is the "mundo loco" of Queca, the prostitute of *La vida breve*, who initiates Brausen (in his assumed character as Arce) into a world which she herself possesses but cannot articulate. Thus the fulfilment of Brausen's potentialities as narrator depends on his excursion into a world of prostitution and madness from which he eventually (unlike Queca) emerges with a fully created fiction. Queca, on the other hand, dies violently, and her death initiates the final flight which forms the climax of the novel. In *La muerte y la niña*, the one character who is genuinely insane (though her "madness" is of a different order from Queca's) is Angélica Inés Petrus, now mysteriously married to Díaz Grey. In spite of obvious differences, there are certain parallels which suggest that a similar pattern is being worked out. In one of his few references to Angélica Inés, Díaz Grey remarks on the nature of her insanity: "Ella, todos lo dicen, no sabe nada de nada. Pero entiende, o se entiende" (70). In other words, in her madness, like Queca, she has imaginative, though not rational, understanding—the quality through which others (in this instance Díaz Grey) may be able to create "literature".

This impression is confirmed by a later reference to her dreams:

> Mi manera de ayudarla era múltiple. [The narrator is Díaz Grey. A veces le decía entusiasta que jamás vio el mundo puta semejante otras, me mostraba entristecido, no demasiado, por mostrarse lujuriosa, perdida en la impudicia. Acaso nunca llegara a entenderme. Pero siempre se aplastaba los huesos de los brazos contra las costillas, para reír o para llorar. Siempre terminaba feliz, resbalando hasta alguno de sus misteriosos sueños enredados que alguna vez recordaba, o volvía a soñarlo mientras me sujetaba temblando para que yo la escuchara. (131-132)[28]

The parallel here is with the anonymous voices (the mysterious "ellos") which Queca hears in her room, and which, for Brausen, are the embodiment of the private world which she herself is incapable of articulating. Angélica Inés does not die—though it is easy to think of her as condemned to a living death—and her initiatory effect on Díaz Grey is less certain. Though in a sense she is the "creator" of her own dreams, she can never be a "narrator"; she tells her dreams to Díaz Grey, but they are never written down and consequently do not enter into the story. Nevertheless, she provides a dimension which extends Díaz Grey's imagination and which, like his feelings for his daughter, creates a rift in his *persona* through which the possibilities of fiction may enter.

The one real death in the story is that of Helga Goerdel, who dies, presumably, early in her married life, and whose marital relations are barely sketched in. As Josefina Ludmer has observed, the absence of the type of married woman who lives at the centre of a family is a constant feature (and a possible limitation) of Onetti's fiction.[29] Yet, if one thinks in terms of fictional strategies rather than of "real life", the reason for such a limitation becomes clear. As Ludmer herself says: "Los personajes femeninos sólo entran en esta categoría [i.e. that of characters who cannot become narrators]; no escritoras, no narradoras, "otras' por excelencia, son las salidas: dementes, locas, extranjeras, o las no entradas: adolescentes; se niega aquí a la mujer adulta, madre, 'responsable' ".[30] The "differences" of women, in other words, are most marked when they exist at some remove from ordinary social life. It is precisely because they belong to a world which is in some sense alienated that they are able to provide the challenge which the potential narrator must take up. The latter, on the other hand, is by definition a character who is able to move between the worlds of difference and normality and ultimately to find a point of rest between them in the fiction which he is able to create. In *La vida breve*, this point of rest is the imaginary world of Santa María, though in subsequent narratives the pattern is repeated within the imaginary world itself. The women, in each instance, fulfil their function at a cost: if writing is a kind of "salvation", as Onetti's characters often assert,[31] it is a solution from which women are excluded by virtue of their "otherness". To fail to achieve salvation—to be unable to "tell a story"—is to invite destruction; even to compromise with one's "difference" by entering the world of domesticity does not basically alter the situation since for women, at least in Onetti's scheme of things, there is no corresponding process of initiation from which the conditions of fiction could emerge. Thus Helga's virtual suicide takes place, in a more than usually literal sense, for the sake of the fiction: not only in order to advance the plot, as might be the case in a realist novel, but in order to demonstrate what, for the author, is a truth about the nature of fiction itself.

Many readers must have been troubled by the way in which Helga's second child is referred to in the text both as "un niño" and "una niña".[32] In Jorge Malabia's account of her death immediately after the event, the two sexes are juxtaposed quite naturally: "La mató—gritó Jorge—. La mató a medianoche con un varón. Ella había pensado siempre en una hembrita" (59). In the last two chapters of the novel, however, the references fluctuate: (Goerdel) "la concepción de la *hija* asesina" (121); (Díaz Grey) "una mujer muerta por una *niña*" (122); (Goerdel) "Sólo quiero probar que el *niño* no pudo ser mío" (127) (italics mine). And this fluctuation is carried over into the scrutiny of the letter in the final chapter: "se insistía sobre el nacimiento de un *niño*" (132) (the letters, if genuine, must precede the birth); and "la gestación y nacimiento de la *niña* (133) (at this point it is Díaz Grey who is explaining) (italics mine). If one bears in mind the fact that Helga was expecting a daughter, one simple explanation of the apparent inconsistency suggests itself: each time the word "niña" is used, there is a reference, direct or indirect, to the mother ("concepción"; "una mujer muerta por . . ."; "gestación"), so that "niña" could stand for "the child as the mother thought of it". However, such an explanation, though possible, seems to have little to do with the pattern of the story as a whole, to which the title itself forms an important clue.

La muerte y la niña ("Death and the maiden") translates the title of the well-known song by Schubert. The musical allusion in itself may suggest the "discos sacros" of Díaz Grey, possibly the only character in the novel for whom the title would have this connotation. What is clear is that the word "niña" (as in the song) is associated with death—here, the death of the mother, not of the child. (This, of course, is the association which would work for Helga Goerdel, who knew that she would die in childbirth and was expecting a girl.) What is more, it places the child in a pattern which includes Díaz Grey's daughter and the Insauberry girl who is the motive behind Goerdel's first return.

The fact that Díaz Grey has a daughter, not a son, links him in yet another way to the "different" world of women; despite her "facelessness", she appears to belong, like the young violinist with whom Díaz Grey escapes at the end of *La vida breve*, to the class of virginal adolescents through whom "salvation" may be achieved. The presence of the Insauberry girl is more mysterious. In Goerdel's dream, the dead Helga first draws his attention to the twelve-year-old girl ("la niña de los Insauberry") as if she were a substitute for the daughter whom she never had: ". . . la empujaba apenas [it is Bergner speaking], para que se adelantara y fuese inconfundible. Diría que en el sueño, reiterado, crónico, la actitud de la difunta no era la de orden u oferta. Simplemente, mostraba a la niña, quería que el soñador no la olvidara" (99-100). It is only in Bergner's later version of the dream that she offers the girl as a future bride: "Tantos días, noches, de súplica y ruego, tantos sudorosos amaneceres con la difunta empujando la niña, quebrando el silencio al final para ordenar. Siempre vestida de blanco" (106). Bergner persists in this view in the face of Díaz Grey's scepticism: it is the latter who sees the girl in the dream as a daughter to be adopted by Goerdel, whose children are all male, and it is Bergner's anger at what he takes to be a wilful misinterpretation which leads to the final rift between the two men. The scene has other consequences, both for Bergner's relations with Goerdel and ultimately with Brausen, whose "divine" guidance merely brings the Insauberry story to an abrupt and unexplained end. What matters in the present context, however, is that María Cristina Insauberry appears, ambiguously, as a child-bride: both the daughter whom Helga never had and a new version of herself, the woman who was taken by death. And the fact that, in the dream, Helga is dressed in white suggests that she has reassumed a virginal quality—perhaps even that she herself has come to resemble the girl in the song.

The pattern all this creates is a curiously shifting one, as if the word "niña", first established in the title, continued to reverberate outwards through several important areas of the text, without ever presenting a clear-cut meaning. Moreover, there is a sense in which the shifting quality is located in the language itself. On this view, the word-pair "niño"/"niña" would be an example of what Stephen Heath calls "metaplasm", defined as "change or transmutation in a word by adding, transposing or introducing a syllable or a letter".[33] Heath uses the term to describe the way in which a text like Robbe-Grillet's *Dans le labyrinthe* structures itself by means of a constant process of verbal repetition and variation, so that "action", in the normal sense of the word, becomes "the action of the narrative taking possession of itself". The case of "niño"/"niña" is simpler, though its effect could be described in similar terms. Just as the system of inflection of the language concerned makes it possible for "niño" to generate "niña" and other members of the paradigm, so at the level of plot, the same process of modification can be made to create a series of ambiguous relationships whose interplay, and the demands which this makes on the reader's attention, form the true "subject" of the book.

By now it should be clear that *La muerte y la niña* is not so much a novel in the conventional sense as a work in which various traditional ingredients of fiction are reconstituted in such a way that the reader is at a loss to extract from it a separate, describable "meaning". Since the story is constructed with the sort of material which is familiar from other kinds of fiction, certain expectations are created for the reader; yet if he attempts to construe the story according to these expectations—to fill in the deliberate hiatuses, to attempt to reconcile the conflicting details, to assume that every effect has its appropriate cause—he will be mentally writing a quite different novel. Above all, perhaps, he will be assuming a relation to an external reality which the author sets out carefully to destroy. As John Sturrock reminds us in his study of Borges, "the process of fiction (is to) substitute language for the world".[34] *La muerte y la niña* begins with an intrusion into the everyday life of the protagonist—a break with his "normal reality"—and it ends with a return to that reality: "Era ya de mañana quando dejamos de jugar al ajedrez. Me levanté para entreabrir las ventanas y silenciar el andante de Bach" (135).[35] In between, a story has been told which offers its own kind of reality, to experience which is ultimately to submit to the permutations of language itself. These permutations have nothing to do with "the truth": all stories, even those based on recollections of "fact", have a tendency to become "tall stories", attempts to cover gaps in what is known to be true. Words themselves may sometimes tell the truth, but more often than not, as Goerdel recognizes, they are used to deceive: "Como usted escucha, doctor, estoy usando el mismo lenguaje que le sirve a usted para mentir. Sin ofensa. Todos mentimos, aún antes de las palabras. Por ejemplo, yo le digo mentiras y usted miente escuchándolas" (124).

At an early stage in the novel, Goerdel and Bergner are accomplices in lying: they consciously take part in a game of mutual deception whose rules they scrupulously observe. This collocation of lying and gameplaying can hardly be fortuitous: all through *La muerte y la niña* there are implied parallels between games and the making of fictions. Both, obviously, take place at one or more removes from reality; both depend on a combination of chance and choice, and both are attempts to keep time at bay. In the two examples I have already mentioned—the game of mutual deception between Goerdel and Bergner and Díaz Grey's game with the photographs —the analogy is clear: in the first, the protagonists tell stories to one another (both sins and forgiveness are "inventions") to conceal the separate egotisms which would destroy their relationship; in the second, Díaz Grey attempts to shut out a reality which may be even more painful, because less ordered, than the fiction he has constructed.

The most revealing example of all, however, is what might be termed the "game with history", since this gives a clue as to how the novel itself should be read. In Chapter XI, just before his final encounter with Goerdel, Díaz Grey reflects on his poor performance in History as a student:

> La falla estaba en que no era capaz de relacionar las fechas de batallas militares o políticas con mi visión de la historia que me enseñaban o intentaba comprender. Por ejemplo: desde Julio César a Bolívar todo era para mí una novela evidente pero irrealizable. Innumerables datos, a veces contradictorios, se me ofrecían en los libros y en las clases. Pero yo era tan libre y tan torpe como para construir con todo eso una fábula, nunca creída del todo, en la que héroes y sucesos se unían y separaban caprichosamente. Napoleón en los Andes, San Martín en Arcola.
>
> Siempre sentía la reiteración: los héroes y los pueblos subían y bajaban. Y el resultado que me era posible afirmar, lo sé ahora, era un ciento o miles de Santas Marías, enormes en gente y territorio, o pequeñas y provinciales como ésta que me había tocado en suerte. Los dominadores dominaban, los dominados obedecían. Siempre a la espera de la próxima revolución, que siempre sería la última (117-118).

Díaz Grey's account of history, clearly, is based on fictional terms: he cannot relate dates ("facts"/"reality") to his vision of history as a novel. (Consequently, if history is a fiction, then facts must lose their "real" status before they can enter into the fiction.)[36] Thus he constructs a "fable" in which events and people combine or separate by a kind of poetic logic which overrides the normal logic of cause and effect. The "fable", moreover, is repetitive (it does not progress); it is also representative of fiction as a whole, since the imaginary world on which it is based—Santa María—is one microcosm among many. Finally, therefore, if people live in hope of an ultimate revolution which would break the pattern of repetition, this, by contrast, would constitute a linear development—the kind of "progress" of which Díaz Grey is sceptical, both in real life and, by implication, in fiction.

Thus, in Díaz Grey's view of history, the barrier between reality and fiction would be irremediably blurred. It would not collapse entirely— fiction is always to some extent a break with external reality, though it makes use of that reality for its own purposes—but its ambiguous nature would ensure the continual production of multiple meanings. In fiction itself, these meanings are an intrinsic part of the activity of reading the text: they are not imported from outside, however much they may appear to feed on external reality; nor can they be gathered into a single, detachable, "meaning". To read *La muerte y la niña* with the kind of attention it demands is to recognize that, instead of "reading the book for the story", we are pursuing the traces of several, sometimes contradictory, stories, in order to arrive at the sense of a text whose justification, quite simply, is its own existence. Or as Gabriel Josipovici has put it, in a not dissimilar context: "As with a Cubist painting, the reader is forced to move again and again over the material that is presented, trying to force it into a single vision, a final truth, but is always foiled by the resistant artefact".[37] To compel us to resist the imposition of a false unity, by reminding us that the products of language themselves are man-made, not natural, arrangements is perhaps the most urgent task of contemporary fiction-writers, and it is one to which Onetti continues to make his own distinctive and splendidly intelligent contribution.

ARTHUR TERRY

Essex

NOTES

[1] Quoted in Fernando Aínsa, *Las trampas de Onetti*, Montevideo, 1970, p. 36.

[2] Cf. Jean Ricardou, *Le Nouveau Roman*, Paris, 1973, p. 121: "Ce qui, dans un texte, se prétend réel, n'est jamais qu'une fiction au même titre que ce qui se prétend fiction".

[3] All page references are to the first edition (Editorial Corregidor, Buenos Aires, 1973).

[4] Fredric Jameson, *The Prison-House of Language*, Princeton, 1972, p. 195.

[5] This situation is modified on p. 15, when Goerdel assumes that Díaz Grey will write him a prescription, but the latter refuses. The comparison here is with the confessor, who does not write prescriptions either.

[6] Cf. "Camina desganado contando al mundo su futuro crimen, asosinato, homicidio, uxoricidio (alguna de esas palabras cuando el Destacamento de Policía se acuerda de mí, cuando necesita al médico forense) . . ." (p. 10) and "Y así nos va convirtiendo a todos en sus testigos de cargo y descargo . . ." (p. 10).

[7] There is a parallel here with Helga Goerdel's equally mysterious visits to Díaz Grey at the beginning of Chapter II (pp. 21-22).

[8] There is an echo of "cálculo" a moment later, when we are told that Goerdel "pareció *contar* en silencio y quietud mientras Díaz Grey hablaba" (p. 14, my italics). The ambiguity here (Goerdel is "calculating", but may also be "continuing his story" in silence) is repeated later (p. 95), when Goerdel is referred to as a "contador"—both a "keeper of accounts" and a "teller of stories".

[9] Josefina Ludmer, *Onetti: los procesos de construcción del relato*, Buenos Aires, 1977, p. 124. This is the most serious study of Onetti's fictional methods so far to have appeared, and one to which I am greatly indebted.

[10] Ludmer, op. cit., p. 184.

[11] Díaz Grey actually originates as a projection of Brausen himself. Cf. "Entraría sonriente en el consultorio de Díaz Grey-Brausen ...", *Obras completas*, Mexico City, 1970, p. 458.

[12] In Onetti, for reasons I shall explain later, women as a whole neither write nor narrate. Informants are those who, in Josefina Ludmer's words: "extraen los datos de un modo directo (de primera mano); son intermediarios entre los hechos de 'la realidad' y el narrador, que los organiza" (op. cit., p. 168). She also points out (p. 168, n. 20) that Onetti's informants tend to be degraded by their contact with "reality". Jorge Malabia, as he appears in *La muerte y la niña*, is a case in point: once a writer (of poems), he has now abandoned his literary ambitions and has succumbed to the crude patriotism which Díaz Grey finds so repugnant.

[13] In *La vida breve*, he is described as "un borroso médico de cuarenta años" (*Obras completas*, p. 442); in *El astillero*, he is nearly fifty, still unmarried and apparently childless; in *La muerte y la niña*, he is simply "(un) anciano" (p. 54) and now has a teenage daughter.

[14] In *La vida breve*, Brausen states quite bluntly: "Pero no interesaba el pasado del médico, su vida anterior a su llegada, el año anterior, a la ciudad de provincias, Santa María" (*Obras completas*, p. 443).

[15] In *El astillero*, Díaz Grey warns Larsen that it would be dangerous for Angélica Inés to have children: "Es duro de decir, pero sería mejor que no tengan hijos" (*Obras completas*, p. 1120).

[16] Cf. Ludmer, op. cit., p. 174, n. 27: ". . . . los narradores de Onetti se encuentran siempre en una situación análoga a lo narrado: en *Los adioses*, el tuberculoso narra al tuberculoso (sobre el personaje tuberculoso), en *La muerte y la niña* son todos 'padres' . . .".

[17] Though Bergner "dies" in an earlier novel and is alive in this one, there is some doubt as to whether he is dying or not, as Malabia suggests in Chapter X: "Prometió verlo a usted, no quiere saber nada con mi tío Bergner, moribundo o sano" (p. 122). At various points in *La muerte y la niña*, it is as if a special *tempo* of ageing were imposed on the fictional characters, who, nevertheless, are not exempted from death. Cf. the reflection which opens Chapter IX: "No nos estaba permitido envejecer, deformarnos apenas, pero nadie impedía que los años pasaran, señalados con festejos, con el escándalo alegre y repugnante de la inmensa mayoría que ignoraban—a veces podía creerse en un olvido—que los burócratas de Brausen los habían hecho nacer con una condena de muerte unida a cada partida de nacimiento" (p. 91).

[18] The same combination of qualities occurs in the updated version of the Cain-Abel story which ends Chapter V, where Brausen acts with the brutal cynicism of a "caudillo político" (p. 60), but finally lapses into indifference, "ahora insignificante, nunca amistoso pero ya lánguido, tal vez, también él, soñoliento" (p. 62).

[19] At the beginning of the novel, Díaz Grey speaks of praying to "Padre Brausen que estás en la Nada". Thus, Brausen is a god whose realm is "la Nada"—the "nothingness", one might claim, from which fiction itself is created.

[20] One of the most curious references to Brausen occurs in Chapter XI: ". . . el crepúsculo que empezaba a devorar la luz de todos los días que nos repetía Brausen, Juan María, casi Junta para los ateos" (p. 120). The implication seems to be that, for those who do not believe in the "divinity" of Brausen, the latter would be something like the equivalent of Junta (the Larsen of *Juntacadáveres* and *El astillero*), that is to say, a kind of "failed artist".

[21] Cf. Ludmer, op. cit., p. 47, n. 4: "Las narraciones de Onetti se producen en el interior de la concepción clásica del relato, aunque con multitud de operaciones de distanciamiento de este esquema . . .".

[22] Stephen Heath, *The Nouveau Roman: a Study in the Practice of Writing*, London, 1972, p. 34.

[23] John Sturrock, *Paper Tigers: the Ideal Fictions of Jorge Luis Borges*, Oxford, 1977, p. 127.

[24] Cf. Ludmer, op. cit., on *Para una tumba sin nombre*: "A partir de allí [i.e. the death of Rita], *Para una tumba* cuenta indefinidamente cuentos; reitera cuentos (mentiras, versiones) que intentan conjurar el vacío original. . . Si Rita 'no cuenta más el cuento', sı la muerte consiste en 'no contar', hay que desencadenar—por inversión, por negación —un mecanismo que, como el de Scherazada, postergue la condena" (pp. 161-162).

[25] On the possible relation between the physical amputation which Gertrudis undergoes at the beginning of *La vida breve* and the "compensatory" origins of the narrative, see the opening section of Josefina Ludmer's study "Homenaje a 'La vida breve' ", op. cit., pp. 18-36.

[26] On the significance of the game of patience and the "discos sacros", see David Musselwhite, "El astillero en marcha", *Nuevos aires* IV, no. 11 (1973), 3-15 (p. 8). For Musselwhite, the "discos sacros" represent "un orden familiar, como el correr de las estaciones y de la vida", in contrast to the "barajar de las alternativas, los órdenes y sistemas provisionales que pueden compararse con las 'recordaciones y deformaciones' de la estructura narrativa". It is perhaps significant that, in *La muerte y la niña*, the game with the photographs replaces the game of patience "con una regularidad cíclica" (p. 77).

[27] At the beginning of the last chapter, Díaz Grey tells how his daughter has finally returned to Santa María, and that he has introduced her to Jorge Malabia: "traté de reunirlos sin un propósito determinado, sólo por la curiosidad, casi científica, de verlos, en lo que me fuera posible, reaccionar" (p. 131). And he adds: "Acaso ésta no sea otra historia". This final sentence could mean several things: (i) perhaps it is a story Díaz Grey will never tell; (ii) perhaps it belongs to the same story (but in what sense?); (iii) perhaps there will be no "story". If the latter, it may be because the daughter has become "una persona" in the sense I have just described.

[28] There is a curious echo here of the connection between madness and prostitution in the reference to Angélica Inés's "shamelessness" and in the (admittedly metaphorical) use of the word "puta".

[29] It is noticeable that, in *La vida breve*, Brausen values the sterility of Queca, whereas he is repelled by Raquel, his sister-in-law, when he finds that she is pregnant.

[30] Ludmer, op. cit., p. 121.

[31] At one point in *La vida breve*, Brausen reflects: "Cualquier cosa repentina y simple a suceder y yo podría salvarme escribiendo", *Obras completas*, p. 456.

[32] The only critic I have come across who refers to this discrepancy is José de la Colina, who speaks of "algún descuido (¿cuidado descuido?), como el de ese niño recién nacido que páginas después es niña" (*Plural* IV, no 1, 1974, 73). I have assumed that the effect is deliberate.

[33] Heath, op. cit., p. 147. The phrase quoted in the next sentence occurs on p. 149.

[34] Sturrock, op. cit., p. 26.

[35] As Josefina Ludmer has observed, the window symbolism is particularly evident in Chapter IV, which describes the crucial discussion between Bergner and Goerdel: "El punto más antinaturalista (menos referencial) de la escritura de Onetti se encuentra en *La muerte y la niña*: 'Bergner fue separándose de la opacidad gris de la ventana' (p. 41); 'Después miró la ventana ciega por la lluvia' (p. 45); 'mirando la ventana negra' (p. 49). Sólo se ve la ventana; no hay nada 'más allá'; el vidrio—el lenguaje y la escritura —es ya la única realidad *contra* 'la realidad' " (op. cit., p. 160).

[36] Cf. the passage on the unimportance of facts which can be checked (p. 32), quoted above, p. 150.

[37] Gabriel Josipovici, "Modern literature and the experience of time", in Josipovici (ed.) *The Modern English Novel, the Reader, the Writer and the Work*, London, 1976, 252-272 (p. 264).

VI

YO EL SUPREMO:
THE DICTATOR AND HIS SCRIPT

> "Para mí sola nació don Quijote, y yo para él: él supo obrar, y yo escribir; solos los dos somos para en uno..."(Cervantes, *Don Quijote de la Mancha*).
>
> "Los dictadores cumplen precisamente esta función: reemplazan a los escritores, historiadores, artistas, pensadores, etc." (Nota final del compilador: *Yo el Supremo*).
>
> "El artista más revolucionario sería aquel que estuviera dispuesto a sacrificar hasta su propia vocación artística por la Revolución" (Fidel Castro, *Palabras a los intelectuales*).

The publication of *Yo el Supremo* in 1974 was an exceptional cultural phenomenon. It was recognised at once as an important and challenging work, both for its own literary worth and for what it appeared to represent within recent Latin American writing. It seemed to arrest the impending decline and fall of the "new" Latin American novel, and its author, Augusto Roa Bastos, who, so it was said, had not previously shown signs of renewing either the forms or the contents of Latin American fiction, now appeared to have achieved both objectives in a novel which constituted a vast watershed, incorporating all the currents of the past and opening out a whole network of new channels into the future. It was more immediately and unanimously acclaimed than any novel since *Cien años de soledad*, and critics seemed to suspect that its strictly historical importance was far greater than that of García Márquez's extraordinarily successful creation, whose optical illusion —the confusion of a bourgeois nationalist consciousness with a socialist consciousness under the mistaken belief that anti-imperialism is the same as anti-capitalism—provides a fitting symbolic image of the "new" novel of the 1960's in general. Obviously, then, it will be a very long time before we have come to terms with Roa Bastos' remarkable work. Yet it is already clear that the novel's central problematic has not been perceived by the majority of critics, and several false starts have been made. It would be a foolish reader indeed who would claim, at this early date, to have produced a definitive interpretation of the structure and meaning of such a book; and yet, it seems possible to argue that this novel's basic *intentions* are remarkably clear and that, if they have not so far been recognised, this is because the conclusions to which they lead are unacceptable to the great majority of writers, critics and other intellectuals concerned with the problems of contemporary Latin America.[1] This study seeks to sketch out an approach to the novel which will establish the outlines of the literary and historical conjuncture within which the work is situated, and to suggest what its place might turn out to be in the development of Latin American literature.

I myself believe that this novel is comparable only to Sarmiento's *Facundo: civilización y barbarie* (1845), both in its peculiar heterogeneity and its historical significance. I believe also that it is the literary work which finally closes the era which *Facundo* itself opened, definitively reversing the signs of Sarmiento's work and completing a long trajectory of novels from *Los de abajo* through *La vorágine, Huasipungo, Hombres de maíz, Pedro Páramo* and *La Casa Verde*, each of which, in differing ways, subjects the idealist values of European "civilisation" to a materialist critique. *Facundo* itself, although an essay, has proved impossible to omit from courses on Latin American literature because of its peculiar method of confronting a social and historical phenomenon through the techniques and perspectives of the creative imagination.[2] Arrogant as he was, and despite his flights of fancy, Sarmiento was constrained by the essay genre to adopt an objectively humble and essentially historical approach to the life and significance of his protagonist, and it is this stance which Roa Bastos emulates in his own creative biography of the great Paraguayan dictator, El Supremo;[3] whereas, it need hardly be said by now, the most recent Latin American fiction has been characterised not so much by humility as by vanity and even narcissism in the most extreme cases (those that consider that "linguistic experimentation for its own sake" is the true path of the novel).[4] *Yo el Supremo*, like *Facundo*, has a very Latin American specificity, and although it is informed by most of the important intellectual currents of our age—an advantage denied to Sarmiento, who was writing, moreover, within ten years of the death of his principal character, while the Other, Rosas, was still alive— and although its universal dimension is never hard to find, it can not in any respect be separated from that specificity. Thus, while it is certainly a novel about dictatorship both as a universal and as a general Latin American problem, it takes its concrete force from, and continually returns to, the life and works of José Gaspar de Francia, the dictator of Paraguay from 1814 to 1840; and although it considers the function and meaning of writing in Western history as a whole, and the roles and duties of the Latin American writer since Independence, it cannot for a moment be separated from the predicament of one specific writer, Roa Bastos himself, confronted with the dilemma of what to write, for whom to write, and whether in any case writing is anything other than an irrelevant or even cowardly thing to do in a continent where dictators are everywhere in power and where the great mass of the population is illiterate and condemned by uneven development to a consciousness anterior to that which has historically produced the novel as a literary form.[5] The question, put very crudely, is this: does the practice of writing fiction have anything at all to contribute to the process of national and continental liberation? Or is the writer condemned, perhaps fatally, to be on the other side?

Seen in this light, it would not be surprising if Roa Bastos were frustrated and disappointed with the reaction to his novel, despite the critical acclaim with which it has been greeted. The fact is that critics have not, in general, perceived the underlying problems to which this novel's structure offers provisional solutions and avenues into the future;[6] have failed to recognise the thematic continuity between *Yo el Supremo* and the Paraguayan novelist's first and seriously underrated novel, *Hijo de hombre*, whose central problematic—the gulf between the intellectual and the *pueblo*, writing and reality, theory and practice—is precisely the same as that of the later and still more radical work, in which the link between the novel as a historical form and the development of bourgeois individualism is explored; and appear to have ignored Roa Bastos' own unequivocal statements on both politics and writing made both before and after the 1974 novel.[7] While a comparison with *Hijo de hombre* and an examination of Roa Bastos' more general pronouncements will by no means solve all the problems which this novel presents, they will unquestionably eliminate certain non-problems which have engaged the attention of a number of critics, such as the extraordinary idea that the book is—simply—a condemnation of Francia,[8] or that it is a mere open-ended exploration of Latin American history and of fictional form.

One of the problems which *Yo el Supremo* has had to surmount is that it is condemned both by its subject matter and its date of publication to comparison with two other novels, Alejo Carpentier's *El recurso del método* (1974), and García Márquez's *El otoño del patriarca* (1975). Although the three writers belong to three different literary generations, they are all known to support the Cuban Revolution (Carpentier, of course, actually represents it), and this fact has complicated the critical perception of their three anti-dictatorial novels. For the unhappy fact is that while both Carpentier's and García Márquez's works appear to be profoundly revolutionary in content, their extremely conservative approach to form—a non-problematic presentation of character and history—reveals disturbingly contradictory underlying ideologies in each case; whereas Roa Bastos, whose apparent scepticism is actually carefully limited, definitely specific, and completely self-aware, is in fact subjecting the form of the novel to an interrogation in order to lay bare its normal ideological function within Western society in the last five hundred years, namely to teach people to distinguish between "truth" and "fiction". What the novel does not, of course, normally reveal to us, is its *structural* allegiance to a class—the bourgeoisie—, and it is this particular problem which consumes Roa Bastos. The purpose of *Yo el Supremo* is to question whether the space of the novel, which is, precisely, the space between YO and ÉL, thought and action, theory and practice, can be used for any purpose other than to consolidate the hegemony of the bourgeois conception of history.

Critics who support the Cuban Revolution, such as Ángel Rama and Mario Benedetti, surely two of the most perceptive writers on Latin American literature in this last decade, appear to have been misled by their allegiance to that revolutionary process into interpreting the novels of Carpentier and García Márquez on the strength of their extra-literary postures, and to have neglected to consider whether those works are in fact "revolutionary" in any convincing sense of the word.[9] It is an unfortunate fact, however, that novelists who support revolutionary movements can write novels which reveal that their unconscious ideology is profoundly contradictory and even reactionary. And this applies more to the novel than to any other literary form because the contradictions which give the novel its unique dynamism are, precisely, the contradictions of the bourgeois consciousness.[10] Roa Bastos himself makes clear both in this novel and in *Hijo de hombre* that he accepts the Marxist analysis whereby the development of class society involves the separation of mental and manual labour[11], and this separation, in its turn, at a particular moment in historical evolution, gives rise to the literary form we call the novel.

The structure of the novel is the narration by a contemplative YO of the actions of a less conscious, distanced ÉL, a relationship which we call irony. Equally important, however, is the indirect relation of the novelist, not only to his "fiction", but to "reality" itself, in the first place, and to his unknown audience, the readers, in the second place. The novelist does not "speak", "sing" or "chant", as the poet does in a literary genre wherein the YO represents, not a distance from an ÉL, but the expression or the recuperation, even if only symbolic, of a NOSOTROS. The novelist, despite the conversational tone which he adopted in the more confident days of the nineteenth century in order to naturalise his creations, is above all and by definition a man who *writes*.[12] Furthermore, he is not acquainted with his audience, but reaches them through commercial mediators, and they, the readers, obtain the book through the anonymous agency of the market and consume it in the solitude of their own houses and in the solitude of their own silent individual consciousness. In other words, if the normal relationship of the intellectual with his society is established at the level of theory rather than practice, the relationship of writer to reader is that of any producer to his consumer within the capitalist mode of production. In Latin America, however, the "normal" distance between the novelist and his readers becomes an unbridgeable chasm. Whereas the poet, who sings, chants and speaks, merely has to consider the classic problems of the level of formal and conceptual sophistication in order to determine the class character of his aesthetic construction, the novelist appears virtually condemned to represent only one class, the bourgeoisie. Latin American poets have felt sufficiently able to unite theory and practice as to join revolutionary struggles and take to the hills in recent years, in emulation of some of the greatest names of the Romantic era; but it would be difficult to name many significant novelists who have done so. The poet can create as he goes, wherever he goes, and is not normally tied to a seat and a desk as the novelist is during long months and years, composing vast organic creations in compensation for, or even in order to mask the fragmentation of society and the alienation from it of the writer himself. The abyss between the Latin American novelist and his indigenous, peasant and worker characters, is one of the aspects which gives rise to those central metaphors of the Latin American essay and novel, "solitude", "absence" and "distance". For the intellectual, the world is full of distances, gaps between himself and the world, between himself and the *pueblo*, between language and reality, theory and practice. Such contradictions are the very fabric out of which *Yo el Supremo* is constructed, providing a classic example of the anguished self-consciousness of a writer who would claim to represent the "Third World". The cases of Carpentier and García Márquez are quite different, however.

Both works, *El recurso del método* and *El otoño del patriarca*, are entertaining works of literature by outstanding Latin American novelists, but both fall well below the previous high standards of these two writers, as Benedetti concedes, and seem to point to a decline which appears to be part of a generalised crisis among the "new" novelists.[13] Perhaps the most striking thing about them is that their dictators are not historical figures, but composite and essentially imaginary ones; that they belong not to the present but to the now rather distant past, which they in no way show to be relevant to the present; and that they break the tradition whereby the characterisation of the dictator is oblique or in other ways problematic, without any obvious advantages accruing from such a risky venture. In short, they appear to evade the challenges of the present—one of the bleakest periods in Latin American history—, shy away from the rigours of a genuinely historical interpretation, and eschew the essential structural problem confronting the Latin American novelist, which is that the novel is not so much a "difficult" form in the tradition of Proust, Joyce and Faulkner, for whom the world was essentially meaningless, as a "problematic" form, precisely because the novel is a creation of the European bourgeoisie. They accordingly ignore the Lukácsian recommendation that great men, even fictional ones, should be left off-stage when historical interpretation is involved,[14] and they enter the minds of their dictators at will. For most practical fictional purposes, total omniscience has long been mistrusted, for a number of well-known reasons; and in the particular case of a dictator, who is in any case, by definition, of all men the one whose consciousness is least available to others, that identification which characterises the novel as a literary experience is surely entirely undesirable. Certitude and familiarity are in this case, to say the least, surprising and unwelcome.

It happens that of all the major Latin American novelists of the past 25 years, Carpentier and García Márquez are perhaps the most certain, over the course of their entire literary production, that the world can be denoted and that stories can be simply narrated, whereas Roa Bastos' uncertainty on this self-same subject was the very point of departure of *Hijo de hombre*.

To be sure, both Carpentier and García Márquez, well aware that the whole history of Latin America is a struggle between European forms and American contents, refer to this problem in their best-known narratives; but they have chosen, significantly enough, to incorporate it as part of the content, not the form, of their works. Neither writer has very seriously raised the problems of writing as such, or of the novel as a genre, and in these two works they complacently lord it over their respective dictators, simple fellows in a simple world who appear to represent few interests other than their own and whose very ingenuousness leaves them at times looking almost lovable. Ángel Rama's assertion that the Patriarca and the Primer Magistrado demonstrate that Latin American fiction is now capable of producing genuine characters at long last, is to say the least questionable: firstly, because the characters concerned are themselves non-problematical; and secondly, because there are no other major characters in their novels and there is no complexity of plot, everything springing as a matter of structural necessity from the actions and the point of view of the two despotic protagonists. They can in no sense be conceived as implicit critiques of present repressive regimes in Latin America. Benedetti, in similar vein to Rama, suggests that Carpentier's use of humour and satire to puncture the dignity of the dictator in *El recurso del método*, is a sign of the maturity of the present school of Latin American writing, but it is difficult to accept that laughter is the most adequate response to the actions of Carpentier's murderous tyrant; and, whilst conceding that *El otoño del patriarca* is not a success, he attributes this to García Márquez's use of hyperbole rather than to a possibly mistaken political perspective. Yet there are moments when the reader is tempted to think that the theme of the individualist dictator has attracted these two writers for reasons of nostalgia, a yearning for the days when, on the one hand, the enemy was a simple and straightforward *coronel* or *doctor* imbued with charisma and *machismo*, and not the anonymous, technocratised, neo-fascist enemy of the 1970's; and when, on the other, novels were linear and chronological, and built around a central protagonist who was in some way or another a reflection or representation of his godlike author. In other words, while it is clearly not merely coincidental that these novels appeared when they did, corresponding obliquely to the phenomenon of military totalitarianism in Latin America since the late 1960's, it is equally no accident that they both look back not, as in the case of *Yo el Supremo*, to the Independence period, but to the moment when the Latin American bourgeoisie became fully visible, that is to say, the moment when, but for the ironies of uneven development—the novelists were not yet ready—, Latin American novelists would have been able to write the classic realist-psychological novel. This leaves the two writers reviewing the images of villains who are no longer enemies, characters who can be understood and perhaps forgiven, especially when compared—how could the reader resist it?—with the barbarians of today.[15]

This difficulty is particularly acute in the case of García Márquez's pathetic patriarch, whose lust for power causes him to miss all the fun in life, in contrast with a monolithic *pueblo* which knows reality when it sees it and knows how to live and love, etc. We know what García Márquez means, of course, but the demagogy blinds him to the fact that the *pueblo* too is composed of individuals and that hundreds of thousands of them die at birth or are exploited throughout their average span of 33 years precisely because of this apparently meaningless craving for power. Power over what, the reader finds himself repeatedly inquiring, only to find himself confronted with implicitly metaphysical solutions. It is hard to bear the thought that Chile's Pinochet will some day have a sympathetic, if supercilious book written about him to demonstrate that he was really the alienated one and not his tortured, exiled or murdered victims. Yet this is precisely what García Márquez appears to be suggesting with his portrait of an elephantine dictator condemned to solitude and absurdity. Satire is the last thing needed to deal with Latin American tyranny—unless written and published from within the frontiers of a nation so subjected—, and fantasy seems inevitably trivial in the face of contemporary horrors. The brutal fact is that there is nothing absurd about Pinochet.

What can be concluded from this? Or rather, what would Roa Bastos have to say about it? That the Latin American novelist, whether or not he follows a party line, is not "free" to invent, for he is playing with the images of the lives of his people.[16] Roa Bastos, indeed, is the latest in a line of Latin American writers—Azuela was the first, followed by Rivera, Asturias, Rulfo and Vargas Llosa—, and perhaps the most radical among them all, who have built their existential dilemma into their novels, taking fragmentation as a structural principle instead of speaking with alien voices and donning the mask of organic form. Such writers accept logical discontinuity and the lack of an integrated psychological typology, not as a proof of the innate absurdity of the world, but as a product of a colonial reality. The works of the most linguistically sophisticated "new" novelists would seem to suggest implicitly that in the age of mass communications and rapid transport the problems of uneven development are close to solution, which may be true—*for them*. The cultural gap can now be made to appear invisible thanks to the new technology, and Europe and the United States are now "in" Latin America. But it is arguable that such misconceptions and mystifications have only confused issues still more.[17]

It is to these problems that *Yo el Supremo* addresses itself, consciously and directly, continuing and updating the analysis offered by *Hijo de hombre* as long ago as 1959. Roa Bastos, like Carpentier and García Márquez, enters the consciousness of his dictator, but it would be difficult to accuse him of implying that such an operation is an easy one to carry out: no novelist can ever have wrestled more exhaustingly yet more fairly with a fictional character than Roa Bastos. Besides, El Supremo himself is obsessively aware of the problems of writing history.[18] Similarly, this novel literally teems with puns and other word-games, but does so precisely to demonstrate the cantankerous dictator's conviction, shared by Roa Bastos, that language and literature have been unreliable, treacherous tools, ever since that division of labour took place which gave some men verbal superiority over others as a reflection of the economic superiority of those same men and others over the same—now lower—classes.[19]

Hijo de hombre, like so many other Latin American novels, dramatised the role of one leading protagonist who was a thinly-veiled projection of the novelist himself, the difference being that Roa Bastos was fully aware of this where other novelists are less so.[20] That narrative clearly underlined the gulf between social classes in Paraguay and seemed to imply that a novel, no matter what its subject matter or apparent point of view, was as sure a sign of the concentration of the means of production in a few hands as any of the more material manifestations. A few years earlier Stalin had made the great discovery that language was not a superstructure, to the amusement of many literary critics; but few of them would deny these days that the use of language and its powers is clearly class-based, or that literature itself is a part of the superstructure. The result of this perception is that Roa Bastos is obsessively concerned with two of the central problems of Western literature and thought, namely truth and sincerity. Miguel Vera, the bourgeois intellectual who is the central character of *Hijo de hombre*, lies to himself within his own subjectivity, and betrays the peasant revolutionaries on the objective plane of the narrative.[21] Thus the first question Roa Bastos asks in *Yo el Supremo*, in terms of logical priority, is: can we know the truth? His long, fragmented answer to this question is cautious and sceptical, and already invokes the topic of language and its relation to reality and consciousness.[22] The second question is: if we believe that we know the truth, will we tell it? Both Marx and Freud address themselves to precisely these two questions, and each suggests, in his different way, that most of us cannot know the truth, and indeed, that even if we intuited it, the same or similar reasons to those that caused us to conceal it from ourselves would certainly ensure that we concealed it subsequently from others.[23] These are inevitable questions in a novel about politicians or intellectuals, and of course Francia, heir to the European Enlightenment and confronted by the mythical *tabula rasa* or blank page of Latin American history, was both. They are questions which are considered in a whole host of Latin American novels, in which the author's uneasy conscience is almost the conventional, if unspoken, point of departure.[24] However, there is in fact a third question, which for Roa Bastos is actually the most important of all, and which only he deals with in such complex yet unflinching detail, which is this: if the intellectual can cast off his alienation from the masses and know the truth (doubtful), and is prepared to tell it (still more doubtful), will he also act on it by putting it into practice? For practice, praxis, is the central problematic of both Roa Bastos' novels.[25] It is here where the two great activist belief systems of the past two thousand years, Christianity and Marxism, come into parallel focus. Both were included in *Hijo de hombre*, the first overtly—religion was given a materialist reading—,[26] and the second by implication. Christianity, however, has been superseded as a problem by the time of *Yo el Supremo*, and Marxism becomes virtually explicit through nearly transparent references to revolutionary processes such as the Chinese Revolution and the Cuban Revolution.

It is here that the question of Roa Bastos' point of view with regard to Francia as historical personage and fictional character must be clarified. Contrary to the conclusions of some critics, the presentation of Francia is, in relative terms, an extremely positive one, in line with recent revisions of the nineteenth-century contradiction between so-called "civilisation" and "barbarism".[27] Instead of selling his country to neo-imperialism, as the River Plate republics and Brazil were contemporaneously doing, thereafter to bemoan their distance from the metropolitan centres and their consequent "solitude"—that of a marooned, parasitic bourgeoisie—, Francia forced his countrymen to assimilate the realities of their historical predicament, confirming through his policies the isolation which Spanish colonial rule had already imposed upon them. Thereupon, taking all political power—even fate itself—into his own hands, he set out to construct a true nation rather than a disguised dependency.[28] In his Paraguay there were no landowners, no middle class, no all-white marriages, no generals, no urbanisation, no foreign trade to speak of, no church domination, no discrimination against the Indians, no corruption, no nepotism, no political parties, no elections, no beggars, no hunger, no poverty, no newspapers, no books: in short, no civilisation. In order to justify his right to such ABSOLUTE power over the objective reality of the nation, the Perpetual Dictator in a sense renounces his claim on humanity and converts himself into a totally abstract self-creation. He denies the effect of heredity ("confabulaciones de la casualidad") or of the environment ("gestándome por mi sola voluntad") upon himself, and abstains from all pleasures of the senses in order to carry out his self-appointed task on behalf of the people who gave him *carte blanche*, in the most literal sense of that French expression, by electing him as their Perpetual Dictator. We are thus presented with the strange paradox of the ultimate individualist who proclaims his non-existence as a person through his self-abnegation on behalf of his only nobility, "la chusma laborativaprocreativa". He makes them truly isolated in order to make them self-reliant and independent, instead of allowing the establishment of a relation of dependency which paradoxically has made the rest of Latin America *feel* isolated. And through his advanced and lucid theoretical comprehension of what is now called neo-colonialism, through his unchallengeable moral example and revolutionary integrity, and—above all—through his ruthless and remorseless conversion of theory into practice, the Supreme Dictator of the novel is able to persuade or force the people to accept the forms of his ideas without, however, changing the essential content to the same radical degree.

This is the tragedy of *Yo el Supremo*. It is inevitable that once Francia dies—for no reality is absolute, no human life is perpetual—his successors will be the product of a conflict or contradiction that his authority was able to suppress but not eliminate. With all due respect to the dialectic and to the revolutionary vanguard, Roa Bastos appears to believe that the normal movement of historical change is not that of form or theory "pulling" content or practice along (a phenomenon symbolised in the novel by the capture of the "meteoro-azar" and the idealist conception of the empty skull as the philosophising dictator's "casa-matriz"), but rather that of content bursting through form. This is a not uncharacteristic position for a Third World intellectual suspicious of all imported doctrines which reduce the specificity of non-European or non-modern experience.[29] In parallel fashion, Roa Bastos also appears to believe that the normal progress of literature in the Western world has similarly been that of form running ahead of content in ways which do not necessarily or even normally point the way to the true future of the genre in question. Hence the importance of the symbol of the egg, in contradistinction to the meteor and the empty skull, as an image of the way in which history gestates in the womb of time and cannot be rushed or speeded up without risk of deformations or without some later compensatory slowing-down. It is, perhaps, as close to an image of authentic tragedy as the modern novel is likely to offer us. The Supremo is not, contrary to what some critics have managed to deduce, held up to shame, ridicule or other forms of condemnation, as an easy target for writers and readers who are actually structurally inserted, without being aware of it, into the same system as he is. He is, rather, presented as a model of the best that could be done in his time and place, a man who went as far as it was possible to go in carrying out objectives which may have been possible at the same time elsewhere or in the same place at some later date. Unfortunately, intellectuals themselves, like books, are a material proof of the contradictions of uneven development, and Francia's epic attempt was bound, "in the last analysis", to fail.[30] The failure is materialised, in the novel, in the flock of blind swallows which crash to their doom ("El Diluvio les salió al paso"), and in the strange sexless Siamese twins who begin trekking in to the capital city at the end of the book, images of a people divorced on the one hand from the full totality of natural human-sensuous experience, and divorced on the other from the possibility of developing their own conscious "vision" in order to guide the direction of the Revolution collectively.

So Francia "fails", and the last pages see him burn all his writings before his final restoration to the unspoken objectivity of the history of his people.[31]

It is too soon to say what this structure and conclusion mean, but it is clear that Roa Bastos' novel has important implications for the relation of literature to history in Latin America and of intellectuals to the political process. It is difficult to resist the conclusion that the novel is addressed above all to Roa Bastos' Cuban friends, who are similarly trying to force the hand of history in the face of the imperialist blockade, in which the relation of an individualist leader to a revolutionary collectivity is similarly being worked out.[32] As a matter of fact, it is impossible to understand the full dialectical significance of *Yo el Supremo* without first recognising that the novel contains an implied critique of the "new" Latin American novel, and secondly, and still more important, without recognising that it is structured around two great presences and two great absences. The presences are Francia, the all-powerful Supreme Dictator, the man who is everything, whose every thought and action is translated at once into objective reality, and whose audience is absolutely certain; and Roa Bastos himself, the "compiler" of the book, alluded to within it as a fugitive and a traitor, a writer of fictions and fables, a man whose impact on his country is negligible after thirty years of exile, and whose audience, like that of all novelists, is wholly indeterminate. The two great absences are Stroessner, the current dictator of Paraguay and an example of the worst kind of Latin American tyrant; and Fidel Castro, who may well be the current version of Francia in Roa Bastos' conception, in which case the book would communicate his earnest hope that Cuba and Castro are different from Paraguay and Francia in their respective relations to the Russian Revolution and the French Revolution. Charles III of Spain's slogan, "Todo para el pueblo, nada por el pueblo", although not of course sincere in the case of the Spanish monarch, could easily have been adopted by Francia. Perhaps some—present writer not included—might see connections between it and Castro's dictum: "Dentro de la Revolución, todo; contra la Revolución, nada".

Yo el Supremo, then, is a meditation on the meaning of writing: its relation to slavery at the very roots of civilisation; its one-dimensional inefficiency and its tendency to freeze thought and language themselves.[33] Writing, we see, is always the product of a distance, whether in time (writing is always posterior, always after the event, always petrifies) or in space (it mediates between those who are separated physically or socially). To sit down and write always takes one out of direct social action, and to write novels does so for a very long time, whereas speaking produces exactly the opposite effect. At the same time, writing is a form of power—or at least, it is the shadow of power—,[34] the possession of a rare and specific skill (rhetoric: persuasion and manipulation) which others do not possess and which carries with it a responsibility. That responsibility, Roa Bastos appears to believe, is to the great mass of people who cannot read and write, the people of the Third World. His position is complicated by the fact that he finds himself condemned to write in a pre-revolutionary situation, unsure of the ground—both political and literary—on which he is standing, and unconvinced of his worthiness to "serve the people". His unease is compounded by the intuition that being an exile in residence in the non-socialist world leaves his fantasies and hopes for a better future intact, fertile, the raw materials of a vision not yet produced or—still worse—reduced by the ruthless demystifying machine of dogmatic Marxism. Nevertheless, everything suggests that he accepts the Maoist line of the "struggle on two fronts", that is to say, the constant interpenetration of the literary with the political,[35] in a tradition that is actually that of Latin America in its first Independence period.

Not least among the novel's virtues is its ability to engage with the most influential debates of the modern era, without referring directly to Marx, Freud, the *Nouvelle Critique* or, indeed, to the *nueva novela*, in a novel which for all its modernity somehow manages also to stir echoes of Quevedo, Torres Villarroel, Larra, and *El periquillo sarniento*. Combined with this, but equally implicit, is a superb reading of the other key works of contemporary Latin American literature. The greatest triumph of all, however, is to have found a means of fusing "literary revolution" with "revolutionary literature" in a way that has allowed the novel to be hailed both by the radicals and the aesthetes among Latin American literary critics, thereby, perhaps, putting an end to a long century of debate and opening up another.[36] Now that we have this astonishing achievement to echo that of Sarmiento 130 years ago, it seems possible to propose that the "True History" of Latin American literature may now begin to be written.[37]

Gerald Martin

Portsmouth

Notes

[1] Readers have perhaps been misled by Roa Bastos' peculiar combination of *minimum certainties*, matters not open to discussion—above all that writing and politics are inseparable, and that the physical sufferings of the people are more important than the metaphysical anguish of artists and intellectuals—and more doubtful or *speculative matters*—how can life be made meaningful, how should one write, what language should one use, etc. The best guide to this distinction between basic premises and open discourse is his first novel, *Hijo de hombre*. In the present article, the *text* will attempt to echo the dogmatic aspect of Roa Bastos' thought, whilst the *footnotes* will seek to evoke the elements of plurality.

[2] "¡Sombra terrible de Facundo, voy a evocarte para que, sacudiendo el ensangrentado polvo que cubre tus cenizas, te levantes a explicarnos la vida secreta y las convulsiones internas que desgarran las entrañas de un noble pueblo! Tú posees el secreto: ¡revélanoslo!" (Sarmiento, *Facundo*: Introduction to the 1845 edition). Both Sarmiento and Roa Bastos wrote as anguished exiles; both used their central figures as points of departure for a discussion of the major themes of their national and continental histories.

[3] Fruitful contrasts might be drawn with novels like Cortázar's *Libro de Manuel* (1973) and Puig's *El beso de la mujer araña* (1976); but Roa Bastos' work, which is neither a "documentary novel" nor a "political novel", opens up a completely new way of confronting the problem of literary and political avant-gardes through his understanding of a concept which his novel "articulates" but does not "utter": that of *ideology*.

[4] Cf. the Supremo's comment on his literary contemporaries: "Cuanto más cultos quieren ser, menos quieren ser paraguayos. . . . A ellos no les interesa contar los hechos sino contar que los cuentan" (*Yo el Supremo*, 3rd ed., Siglo XXI, Buenos Aires, 1975, p. 38). And: "Historias de entretén-y-miento. No estoy dictándote uno de esos novelones en que el escritor presume el carácter sagrado de la literatura" (p. 65). The dictator's constant complaint is that writers do not know how to observe and respect the rigours of history.

[5] These problems were dramatised by the character of Miguel Vera in Roa's first novel, but in an important 1971 interview he confessed that they were also his own: "Empecé a escribir empujado irresistiblemente por ese 'clamor incesante' que resonaba en lo hondo de mí como una imposición de mi mala o falsa concienca: la del desertor, la del fugitivo" ("Entretiens avec ARB", *Caravelle*, (1971), 214). In *Yo el Supremo* Francia himself refers to *Hijo de hombre* as "una de esas innobles noveletas" (p. 102) and to Roa Bastos as a treacherous exiled scribe.

[6] The only exception I know of is Alain Sicard, of Poitiers, who, in his perceptive comments on the papers of other critics during the important Poitiers seminar, remarked that the key to understanding the novel is its careful fusion and separation of literature and politics. Perhaps his most important insight, however, is this: "En *Yo el Supremo* hay una crítica de la literatura y una autocrítica del novelista que son constantes" (*Seminario sobre Yo el Supremo de Augusto Roa Bastos*, Centre de Recherches Latino-Américaines, Poitiers, 1976, p. 115).

[7] In addition to the 1971 interview in *Caravelle*, see ARB, "América Latina en MARCHA", *Marcha*, no. 1646 (Montevideo, 8 July 1973, p. 9), and "Entretiens avec ARB", *Les Langues modernes*, LXXI, (1977), 57-62.

[8] Critics as distinguished as Artur Lundkvist and Giuseppe Bellini have come to this conclusion.

[9] See M. Benedetti, "El recurso del supremo patriarca", *Casa de las Américas*, no. 98 (1976), 12-23, and A. Rama, *Los dictadores latinoamericanos* (FCE, Mexico City, 1976). Both writers recognise the excellence of *Yo el Supremo*—Benedetti predicts that it will become a Latin American classic—but tend to stress its apparent pluralism, whereas the clear consensus at the Poitiers seminar was to contrast its radical intentions favourably with the "literariness" of the novels by Carpentier and García Márquez. See esp. the papers by N. Perera San Martín and F. Moreno Turner. See also an interesting review by Michael Wood of the English translations of *El recurso* and *El otoño*, "Unhappy Dictators", *New York Review of Books*, Vol. 23, no. 20 (9 Dec. 1976), 57-8.

[10] This is why Roa Bastos insists that the writer must always be self-aware, in order to struggle against the tides of ideology: "Sentimos la necesidad de *hacer* una literatura que no quede en literatura, de hablar contra la palabra, de escribir contra la escritura: una literatura que exprese, en suma, en un amplio despliegue de matices y posibilidades, el mundo de la identidad personal de sus autores en consonancia con la identidad del contexto real al que pertenecen" (*Caravelle*, p. 218).

[11] The key text here is *The German Ideology*, where Marx and Engels argue that with the d. of l. consciousness can "flatter itself that it is something other than consciousness of existing practice" and can "emancipate itself from the world" and proceed to the realm of "pure" theory, producing a situation in which "intellectual and material activity—enjoyment and labour, production and consumption—devolve on different individuals" (*The German Ideology*, Part One, ed. C. J. Arthur, London, 1974, p. 52).

[12] "Separados de su pueblo por accidente o por vocación, descubren que deben vivir en un mundo hecho de elementos ajenos a ellos mismos con los cuales creen confundirse. Se creen seres providenciales de un populacho imaginario" (*Yo el Supremo*, p. 23).

[13] This is the view of Jean Franco in an important recent article, "From Modernization to Resistance: Latin American Literature 1959-1976", *Latin American Perspectives*, no. 16 (Winter 1978), 77-97. She too sees *Yo el Supremo* as an exception and comments that it "reveals history as something which is produced and not a given or eternal truth" (p. 94).

[14] This dictum was observed by Asturias in *El señor Presidente* (in which Estrada Cabrera's appearances are strictly limited), by Fuentes in *La muerte de Artemio Cruz* (in which Calles momentarily appears), and by Vargas Llosa in *Conversación en la Catedral* (in which Odría is similarly kept out of view).

[15] Carpentier himself, in *Los pasos perdidos* (1953), had said that Pancho Villa's barbarous misdeeds were like "alegres estampas de novela de aventura", in comparison with the inhuman brutality of European civilisation in its 20th-century wars.

[16] In his 1973 article in *Marcha*, Roa Bastos refused, for similar reasons, to discuss his own life and work: "a mi juicio, resulta superfluo y hasta chocante privilegiar de este modo las opiniones personales, sobre todo de los escritores que trabajan en el campo de la literatura de ficción".

[17] "Profetizaron convertir a este país en la nueva Atenas. Areópago de las ciencias, las letras, las artes de este Continente. Lo que buscaban en realidad era entregar el Paraguay al mejor postor" (*Yo el Supremo*, p. 10).

[18] Large sections of the novel reproduce the chronicles of foreigners who have distorted the image of Paraguay and Francia in their own interests, in addition, of course, to Francia's irate rebuttals. This theme has long been an obsession of Roa's: "La dificultad de una 'lectura' correcta de la realidad paraguaya se ve agravada por la enorme confusion que han producido las antojadizas interpretaciones de sociólogos e historiadores nacionales y extranjeros que han hecho de la 'culturología' paraguaya una actividad que pareciera atacada de sonambulismo o de delirio" (*Caravelle*, no. 17, p. 208). In a recent article, E. Bradford Burns has shown that "Latin America's written memory consists largely of a limited socially constructed reality" ("Ideology in 19th C. Latin American Historiography", *HAHR*, vol. 58, 3, 1978, 409-431. Quotation p. 409).

[19] "The production of ideas, of conceptions, of consciousness, is at first directly interwoven with the material activity and the material intercourse of men, the language of real life. Conceiving, thinking, the mental intercourse of men, appear at this stage as the direct efflux of their material behaviour" (Marx and Engels, *The German Ideology*, p. 47).

[20] Vera's biography was very close indeed to that of Roa Bastos, which makes his epitaph in that novel particularly interesting: "un ser exaltado, lleno de lucidez, pero incapaz en absoluto para la acción. Pese a haber nacido en el campo, no tenía la sólida cabeza de los campesinos, ni su sangre, ni su sensibilidad, ni su capacidad de resistencia al dolor físico y moral. . . . Le horrorizaba el sufrimiento, pero no sabía desprenderse de él. Se escapaba entonces hacia la desesperación, hacia los símbolos" (*Hijo de hombre*, Casa de las Américas, Havana, 1970, p. 389).

[21] "Yo era muy chico entonces. Mi testimonio no sirve más que a medias. Ahora mismo, mientras escribo estos recuerdos, siento que a la inocencia, a los asombros de mi infancia, se mezclan mis traiciones y olvidos de hombre, las repetidas muertes de mi vida. No estoy reviviendo estos recuerdos; tal vez los estoy expiando" (*Hijo de hombre*, p. 11).

[22] Essentially Roa accepts Marx's view of language as "practical consciousness".

[23] Thus Roa insists that his own work is an ideological construct, even beyond the limits of his own awareness: "Lo que no se podrá pasar por alto, sin duda, es su significado ideológico: de este núcleo irradia o a él converge la red de significaciones posibles. Sabemos también que si bien la obra no es la ideología, ésta se halla presente no como reflejo sino como irradiación de la escritura hasta en las fantasías más destiladas" (*Les Langues modernes*, LXXI, 1977, 58-9).

[24] Examples are Asturias's *El señor Presidente*, Vargas Llosa's *La ciudad y los perros* and *Conversación en la Catedral*, and most of Onetti's works.

[25] "The philosophers have only interpreted the world, in various ways; the point, however, is to change it" (Marx, *Theses on Feuerbach*, XI). See also Mao Tsetung, "On Practice". In *Hijo de hombre* the peasants are unafraid of death: "Se sienten vivir en los hechos. Se sienten unidos en la pasión del instante que los proyecta fuera de sí mismos. . . . No hay otra vida para ellos. No existe la muerte. Pensar en ella es lo que corroe y mata. Ellos viven simplemente" (p. 389). The supreme example was Cristóbal Jara: "Ir abriéndose paso en la inexorable maraña de los hechos, dejando la carne en ella, pero transformándolos también con el elemento de esa voluntad cuya fuerza crecía precisamente al integrarse en ellos." (p. 349). The Supremo in the later novel comments that the people are real, whereas intellectuals and politicians are merely "seres probables" mounted on ideas which must be converted into reality. Hence his rule: "Hacer cumplir lo hablado, lo escrito, lo pactado, lo firmado".

[26] "Era un rito áspero, rebelde, primitivo, fermentado en un reniego de insurgencia colectiva. . . . La gente de aquel tiempo seguía yendo año tras año al cerro a desclavar al Cristo y pasearlo por el pueblo como a un víctima a quien debían vengar y no como a un Dios que había querido morir por los hombres" (*Hijo de hombre*, p. 10).

[27] The 1977 interview in *Les Langues modernes* leaves no room for doubt as to Roa Bastos' profound admiration for Francia, "el director civil y político del proceso de la independencia del Paraguay", creator of "un socialismo de estado de características muy peculiares". The interview makes essential reading.

[28] Francia sets out in the novel to restore "la soberanía del Común" thanks to his absolute possession of "el verbo de la Independencia".

[29] This position is justified by the attitudes of many Marxist thinkers, who, unlike Marx himself, rarely take "human-sensuous activity" into consideration (see *Theses on Feuerbach*, I), proving once again that orthodoxy and dogmatism are by no means the same thing. The world of sexuality and emotion is, so to speak, a closed book to the Supremo (see esp. the episode with "Deyanira-Andaluza", and the criticisms of him made by his dog Sultán and his Negro valet, Pilar, both of course closer to Nature than he is). One might say, paraphrasing Senghor, that "emotion is indigenous". Francia himself says: "Lo único nuestro es lo que permanece indecible detrás de las palabras. Está dentro de nosotros" (p. 445). Roa Bastos has accepted that a psychoanalytic reading of *Yo el Supremo* would produce illuminating results (*Les Langues modernes*, p. 61).

[30] The nature of his failure appears to prove that the craving for absolute power is a projection of the idealist desire to live for ever.

[31] Francia returns in death to the "Etnia de mi Raza", reminding us at the end that writing is less significant than the least significant act (p. 219).

[32] On p. 434 we discover that one Francisco Solano López is in a school called "Escuela No. 1, 'Patria o Muerte' ", and on p. 351 that Paraguay is the first "Patria Libre y Soberana de América del Sur". Similarly, the title given to Francia, "Piloto-de-Tormentas", recalls that of Mao Tsetung, "The Great Helmsman". This apart, the later sections of the novel are full of theorising about revolutionary strategy in the Third World context.

[33] Hence references to "el son-ido" and to "la pesada escritura que ya nos ha atrasado millones de años" (p. 66). "Yo sólo puedo escribir; es decir, negar lo vivo. Matar aún más lo que ya está muerto" (p. 102). "Las formas desaparecen, las palabras quedan, para significar lo imposible. Ninguna historia puede ser contada. . . . Mas el verdadero lenguaje no nació todavía" (p. 15). The Supremo's manichean "Rayo de la rectitud", which turns everything into black and white (p. 440), is the dialectical opposite of his earlier "Portapluma-recuerdo" (pp. 214-219), which had passed into the hands of the "compiler".

[34] "Creo que tener la palabra es sólo tener un poder ficticio; o en todo caso es sólo un poder con relación a la palabra en sí misma en tanto habla o escritura" (ARB, in *Les Langues modernes*, p. 60). See J. King, "*Yo el Supremo*: Dictatorship and Writing in Latin America", *Comparison*, no. 7 (Warwick, Spring 1978), 98-106.

[35] "What we demand is the unity of politics and art, the unity of content and form, the unity of revolutionary political content and the highest possible perfection of artistic form. Works of art which lack artistic quality have no force, however progressive they are politically" (Mao Tsetung, "Talks on Literature and Art at the Yenan Forum", 1942).

[36] Perhaps the key concept is this: "Escribir no significa convertir lo real en palabras sino hacer que la palabra sea real. Lo irreal sólo está en el mal uso de la palabra, en el mal uso de la escritura" (p. 65).

[37] I have just received a copy of ARB's latest publication *Las culturas condenadas* (Siglo XXI, Mexico City, 1978), a collection of anthropological studies of Paraguayan Indian groups "compiled" (once again) by the exiled novelist.

VII

ABADDÓN, EL EXTERMINADOR:
SABATO'S GNOSTIC ESCHATOLOGY

"La mujer no es solamente un instrumento de
conocimiento, sino el conocimiento mismo".
(Octavio Paz.)

Sabato has published only three novels in the past thirty years. These novels have needed, or so it would seem, long gestation periods. In his latest work, *Abaddón, el exterminador*, published in 1974, we are told that since the publication of *El túnel* (1948), but particularly since *Sobre héroes y tumbas* (1961), he has been aware of occult, malignant forces bent on preventing the completion of the new novel: "Durante años debí sufrir el maleficio. Años de tortura" (*A*, 21).[1] This hostility is not a metaphor for some sort of creative difficulty experienced by Sabato, it comes from an "entidad que lucha contra el Sr. Sabato" (*A*, 31)[2] which he believes to be "real". Sabato attributes this hostility to his repeated attempts to investigate and reveal in his fiction the nature and origin of this occult world whose attitude towards him is but a small part of its hostility towards all mankind. *Abaddón* is the result of this quest of Sabato's; the purpose of this essay is to throw some light on the nature and sources of this aspect of the novel and, as a consequence, to suggest an interpretation.

As its title implies, the novel contains Apocalyptic visions that Sabato has been anticipating—or so we are led to believe—since he ceased to be a physicist in the Joliot-Curie Laboratories in Paris before the war. Sabato is neither alone nor original in holding such gloomy views about our future: the Joachite tradition is not dead,[3] and the 1960's, in particular, when Sabato was writing *Abaddón*, saw a revival which is not yet spent of religious and occult literature as well as student demonstrations and Aldermaston marches. In France, Louis Pauwels and Jacques Bergier published a magazine, *Planète*, and a book, *Le Matin des magiciens* (Paris, 1960),[4] in which Sabato found the support he needed for some of his ideas and to which I shall have occasion to return.

I say that he "found support" in this book, because although some passages from *Le Matin*[5] are incorporated verbatim in *Abaddón*, some of Sabato's ideas precede its publication. He has been remarkably consistent in his views, using each new novel, each new essay, to reformulate and elaborate earlier ideas that he considers important. *Abaddón* is, in many ways, a new version of *Sobre héroes y tumbas*, and it is not just a question of the mere reappearance of certain characters, such as Bruno Bassán and "el loco" Barragán. Characters reappear and play leading roles *under new names*. Alejandra is now Agustina and Soledad; Martín is Nacho Izaguirre,

Agustina's brother; Fernando, under the names of Sabato and R., is the natural protagonist; Carlos, of "La fuente muda",[6] is "reincarnated", first in the Carlos of *Sobre héroes y tumbas*, now in *Abaddón* in Palito. Certain capital episodes take place again, like the ritual intercourse between Fernando and his daughter Alejandra, this time between Sabato and Soledad, also under the Church of the Immaculate Conception in Belgrano. This is not by any means an exhaustive list of parallels, but an indication that Sabato considers that the writing of fiction is a task not completed with the publication of one work. This is why he said to Nelly Martínez, talking about *Abaddón*, which he was then writing, that "acaso las obras sucesivas son más bien intentos de profundizar lo que en las precedentes se ha dicho de manera más precaria o superficial".[7] This echoes an earlier opinion: "los más grandes novelistas son poco 'fecundos', si por fecundidad se entiende fabricar grandes cantidades de historias diferentes. Cuanto más profundo es un creador, más insiste sobre una sola obsesión (sería filosóficamente reprochable llamarla 'idea')" (*EF*, 179). In *Abaddón* itself, he writes to an aspiring novelist: "Escribí cuando no soportés más, cuando comprendés que te podés volver loco. Y entonces volvé a escribir 'lo mismo', quiero decir, volvé a indagar, por otro camino con recursos más poderosos, con mayor experiencia y desesperación, en lo mismo de siempre" (*A*, 127). *Abaddón* is thus, in a sense, a "final" word and may, in consequence, be used in the interpretation of Sabato's earlier fiction.[8]

Fernando, as I have just said, becomes Sabato in this novel. Sabato is himself the main character of the novel. The full significance of this will be made clear later; for the moment, only this literary innovation need concern us. He is in the fiction on a par with all the other characters, both real and fictional. His wife, Matilde, referred to as M., and both his children, Jorge Federico (b. 1938) and Mario (b. 1945), are also there, briefly, as are some of his friends. The nature of his role is explained to Silvia, a girl who comes with some young "committed" writers to question him: "Hablo de una novela en que está en juego el escritor. [. . .] No hablo de un escritor en la ficción. Hablo de la posibilidad extrema que sea el propio escritor de la novela esa el que está dentro. Pero no como un cronista, como un testigo. [. . .] Como un personaje más en la misma calidad que los otros que sin embargo salen de su propia alma. Como un sujeto enloquecido que conviviera con sus propios desdoblamientos" (*A*, 276). For this reason, *Abaddón* comes very near to being autobiography, more so than any of his earlier fiction, where already friends and foes could find out who Ernesto Sabato is, as he himself said (*EF*, 51). To Joaquín Neyra he said: "Dada la naturaleza del hombre, una autobiografía es inevitablemente mentirosa. Y sólo con máscaras, en el carnaval de la literatura, los hombres se atreven a decir sus (tremendas) verdades últimas".[9] Writing autobiographical literature is not, for Sabato, a form of self-indulgence. It leads the reader to self-knowledge, since "nadie puede advertir en una obra más de lo que él mismo, al menos en potencia, tiene" (*EF*, 224), and the writer to universal knowledge. Like Heraclitus, who said that every cosmology begins with self-knowledge,[10] Sabato believes that "alcanzamos la universalidad indagando nuestro propio ser" (*EF*, 83).

In conversation with Borges, he denied that he was being merely autobiographical on the grounds that there are cases of obvious fantasy, such as "cuando me transformo en murciélago",[11] but this carries no conviction. This episode may not be factual but, as we shall see later, it is anything but fantasy. Sabato adds, perhaps unwittingly contradicting himself: "mezclé episodios estrictamente realistas al lado de otros completamente fantásticos, porque es la única manera de *hacer creíbles* los fantásticos".[12] Furthermore, the nature of Sabato's beliefs makes it imperative that we should widen as much as possible our concept of literalness. He said to Borges on the same occasion: "Yo creo en los horóscopos cuando están hechos como es debido".[13] "Pero usted no cree, Sabato, que el cielo y el infierno son invenciones verbales?" asked Borges. "Creo que son realidades," replied Sabato, "aunque eso no quiere decir que sean realidades tan candorosas como las que se le enseñan a los chicos en las iglesias".[14] He believes, too, that the soul "pertenece a un orden ontológico distinto: no está ni en el espacio ni en el tiempo astronómico. Si por algún procedimiento puede, aunque transitoriamente, 'salirse' del cuerpo, entonces se pondrá fuera del espacio-tiempo".[15] According to Sabato, this faculty of the soul explains the possibility of premonitions.[16] These and similar beliefs play an important part in *Abaddón*. The biographical elements therefore extend beyond the details of his life story, accurate though they are,[17] to typically occult tenets.

Now the form of the novel, too, is partly dictated by a belief central to occult thinking: the inexistence of what we call "coincidences".[18] Sabato puts it succinctly in an aphorism: "CASUALIDAD. ¿Barbarismo por causalidad?" (*U*, 26).[19] Stated at greater length, it implies that two or more events may be meaningfully linked although they are not causally connected. *Abaddón* abounds in this form of acausal linking, for which I shall use—for convenience, and without pretence at technicality—the term coined by Jung, "synchronicity".[20] There is a fundamental difference between the principles stated by Jung and Sabato: Sabato believes that the link is only *apparently* acausal; what connects the events are the forces which direct human life and which man cannot easily escape.[21] For Jung, on the other hand, a "transcendental cause is a contradiction in terms".[22] In spite of this divergence, Jung's term can be used, because although Sabato's "causality" is transcendental, the contradiction is nowhere apparent. In practice, the two theories deal with similar connections. The term is also useful since it immediately suggests both a difference from and a similarity to simple synchronism.

The novel is divided into two parts (though not so called or numbered by Sabato), and both of these into short and often unconnected sections.

The first part, "algunos acontecimientos producidos en la ciudad de Buenos Aires en los comienzos del año 1973" (pp. 11-18) forms, because of its brevity and content, a sort of introduction. Synchronicity plays a particularly important part in it. It comprises three sections. In the first, "en la tarde del año 1973", Bruno Bassán sees Sabato in the street, not seeing anything or anyone, as if in a trance, having fallen into "lo que él llamaba un pozo" (*A*, 11). In the second, "en la madrugada de esa misma noche", three unconnected episodes are narrated (these will be discussed presently) and, in the third, Bruno Bassán reflects on his role as a "testigo impotente" of all these events, and voices a wish to write a novel about them. The second, very much longer, part of the novel (pp. 21-528) is made up of "confesiones, diálogos y algunos sueños anteriores a los hechos referidos, pero que pueden ser sus antecedentes, aunque no siempre claros y unívocos. La parte principal transcurre entre comienzos y fines de 1972. No obstante, también figuran episodios más antiguos, ocurridos en La Plata, en el París de preguerra, en Rojas y en Capitán Olmos (pueblos estos dos de la provincia de Buenos Aires)". As I have just said, the central section of the first part (pp. 12-14) relates three unconnected episodes. In the first, Natalicio Barragán, "el loco", has a vision of a fire-spitting dragon "cubriendo el firmamento" (*A*, 12).[23] In the second, Nacho Izaguirre has final proof of the sordid affaire between his sister Agustina and Pérez Nassif, her employer. In the third, Marcelo Carranza dies in police custody after days of atrocious torture "por formar parte de un grupo de guerrilleros" (*A*, 14). Sabato is, once more, using the device he used in his previous two novels, namely that of anticipating the outcome of the plot or, in this case, plots, since these three sections are taken up and developed in the closing stages of the novel.

Abaddón thus opens with three unrelated episodes within another three, with one triangle within another. In the present context, I think it would be legitimate to speak of cabbalistic triangles, that is, of significant conjunctions, and synchronicity.[24] Bruno draws our attention to the importance of their occult link: "Estaban no sólo vinculados, sino vinculados por algo tan poderoso como para constituir por sí mismo el secreto motivo de una de esas tragedias que resumen o son la metáfora de lo que puede suceder con la humanidad toda en un tiempo como este" (*A*, 17). But of course, this "vínculo" is neither causal nor explicit. There is more to this opening part: all three episodes add up to the number six, the number of days God took to make the world; Genesis is, appropriately, at the beginning. But six is also the product of three, which is male, and two, which is female; six thus symbolises the "essential principle both of the male who sows and of the female that receives the seed".[25] Two superimposed triangles can also form a star. If we remember that all six events take place on January 6th, Epiphany, when a star guided the Magi to Bethlehem, this suggestion will perhaps seem less far-fetched. Sabato himself draws attention to the ancestry of such interpretations: "Isaac el Ciego es padre de la Cábala moderna. . .

Símbolos, letras y cifras, salen de la magia, de los gnósticos y del Apocalipsis según San Juan. El número 3 en Dante. Hay 33 cantos. Hay 9 cielos. . ." He refers to these remarks as "datos a tener en cuenta" (*A*, 295). I think they have to be taken into account when reading this novel. However, the full significance of the synchronicity of these six events and the day of the year when they occur will become fully apparent only at a later stage in my argument.

The course of the novel is thus set by an implied question: what is the connection between the events of the 5th and 6th of January, 1973? To answer this, to discover the occult link between these private and public events, will be Sabato's endeavour, both inside and outside the fiction. His is, then, a quest for knowledge, a knowledge ultimately locked in the novel.[26] If we pause to consider what the six events have in common, we see that they are all either disturbing, frustrating or tragic, full of gloomy foreboding. But Sabato does not simply infer from these isolated cases man's tragic destiny. He deduces it from a general theory about the world, a true cosmology, already hinted at by Fernando Vidal, which he puts here into the mouth of a minor character, el doctor Alberto Gandulfo, and confirms himself. Sabato believes that "toda filosofía es el desarrollo de una intuición central, hasta de una metáfora: panta rei, el río de Heráclito, la esfera de Parménides" (*A*, 47). His cosmology, too, springs from just such a central intuition, namely the Gnostic belief that the world is evil, since it was not God that made it, but the Devil. "Según los gnósticos el mundo sensible fue creado por un demonio llamado Jehová," explains Sabato after listening to Gandulfo's exposition. "Lo cierto, lo indudable es que el Mal domina la tierra. Claro, no todo el mundo puede ser engañado, siempre hay hombres que sospechan" (*A*, 376). Sabato is, of course, one of them. For the Gnostic, evil is not an abstraction but a reality directly experienced.[27] The struggle causes Sabato the difficulties I mentioned earlier, "maleficios" and "pozos", because "éste es el objetivo del plan satánico: impedirnos que conozcamos la Verdad, evitar así nuestra emancipación" (*A*, 372).

★　　★　　★

The novel moves along two paths which could be called public or historic on the one hand and personal or private on the other, but both chart the progress of evil and therefore converge ideologically at the end of the novel. It would be as well to consider these two in turn, beginning with the public or historic path; by this, I mean those episodes in the novel connected with recent history—the Second World War, the atom bomb, political strife, etc. Sabato interprets historical events in the light of the Gnostic theory I have just sketched. Since he started his career as a physicist, the curious theories that he holds about atomic fission and the last war are of particular interest.

The longest section in the novel (pp. 296-344) is devoted to his stay in Paris in 1938. It is then, as we know from *Abaddón* (p. 297) and from his own declarations,[28] that his mistrust of science and his interest in literature began. Then, too, he unwittingly threw away a chance to know more about the relationship between alchemy and the atom bomb. Two strange visitors came to see him one day in the Joliot-Curie Laboratory, Molinelli, a voluminous occultist friend of Sabato, "una excelente persona" (*A*, 326), who lived in Paris and died in 1971, and a mysterious little man called Citronenbaum. They wanted to discuss nuclear physics and alchemy with Sabato and to talk about a "genuine alchemist" that they admired enormously, Fulcanelli.[29] Unfortunately, Sabato spoiled this promising interview by laughing uncontrollably, and his visitors were offended. Citronenbaum disappeared and refused to meet Sabato again, but Molinelli told Sabato later on something of the purpose of the Citronenbaum visit. Citronenbaum had been sent by Helbronner, the French physicist and "perito en los tribunales" (*A*, 324) to interview Fulcanelli or at least, someone—since his identity was not known—whom they thought was Fulcanelli, "un señor que trabajaba en el laboratorio de la Sociedad del Gas" (*A*, 328).

> Este señor le advirtió que tanto Helbronner como Joliot y sus colaboradores, para no hablar más que de los franceses, estaban al borde de un abismo. Le habló de los experimentos que estaban realizando con deuterio y le dijo que esas cosas las conocían ciertos hombres desde siglos atrás y que por algo habían guardado silencio, archivado todo cuando los experimentos llegaron a cierto punto y relatado lo que sabían en un lenguaje que parecía disparatado, pero que en rigor era cifrado. Le explicó que además ni siquiera eran necesarios la electricidad y los aceleradores, que bastaban ciertas disposiciones geométricas para desencadenar los poderes nucleares" (*A*, 328).

Unlike scientists today, he added, the alchemists, the real initiates, "esa cadena de hombres como Paracelso, o el conde de Saint-Germain y hasta el propio Newton" (ibid.), had a conscience. Furthermore, their real pursuit was not the transmutation of metals, "lo esencial era la transformación del propio investigador" (ibid.). This episode and these quotations are taken by Sabato from *Le Matin* (pp. 160-164), where Bergier, who looks like Citronenbaum and who was still a scientist in the thirties (later he was to renounce his scientific calling), is sent by Helbronner to visit the supposed Fulcanelli at the "laboratoire d'essai de la Société du Gaz de Paris".[30] Bergier's account of his visit, the alchemist's words and his predictions are identical in both books. Sabato transposed what he read in the 1960's in *Le Matin* to his stay in Paris in 1938, for, like Pauwels and Bergier, he wants to "backdate" his concern about nuclear research. Looking at the lead tube containing a radio-active substance, Sabato reflects on the "microscópicas miniaturas del Apocalipsis" (*A*, 344) taking place within it. Molinelli warns him that the end is in sight: "La fisión del uranio. El Segundo Milenio" (*A*, 334); "Ahora después de treinta años vuelven a mi memoria esos días de París, cuando la historia ha cumplido parte de sus funestos vaticinios. El 6 de agosto de 1944 los norteamericanos prefiguraron el horror final en Hiroshima. El 6 de agosto. El día de la Luz, de la Transfiguración de Cristo en el Monte Tabor!" (*A*, 344). But perhaps the most significant remark made by Molinelli is about the true meaning of the then forthcoming war between the Allies and the Axis: people would see superficially the struggle of great powers, but "por detrás de esa apariencia había algo más grave: Hitler era el Anticristo" (*A*, 335).

The connection between Hitler, evil and Sabato's personal troubles which I mentioned at the beginning contains further synchronistic links. The persecution Sabato suffers comes, he thinks, from a German émigré and his companion, Dr Schneider and Hedwig von Rosenberg. Hedwig's dependence on Schneider, her total submission to his will, lead him to think that "entre ellos sólo podía haber la relación de mago a médium" (*A*, 74). Sabato is convinced that Schneider "no es un mistificador de feria sino que verdaderamente está vinculado con potencias tenebrosas". He feels well qualified to assert that fact because "para desenmascarar a esos agentes hay que ser creyente", as he says he is (*A*, 78). His fears are quite specific; Schneider, he says, "me inquietaba por lo que podía hacer conmigo durante el sueño, o en sueños provocados. [. . .] Hay individuos que tienen el poder de provocar el desdoblamiento, sobre todo en los que como yo somos propensos a sufrirlo de modo espontáneo. Al verlo a Schneider, tuve la certeza de que tenía ese poder" (*A*, 77).[31] Schneider, who probably escaped from Nazi Germany after the war, like Eichmann and Mengele, also bears the name (common enough in German, admittedly) of a medium famous in the 1920's and '30's, Rudi Schneider. Maybe this is "coincidence" rather than synchronicity, but there is more, for Rudi Schneider and his brother Willi were born in Braunau-on-Inn, Salzburger Vorstadt, where Hitler was born. Now the nationality, profession and place of birth of Rudi Schneider obviously suited the character in Sabato's novel—the reason, I suggest, why Sabato chose the name.[32]

Hedwig also bears an interesting surname. She is made to belong to the Rosenberg family, as "la condesa Hedwig-Marie-Henriette-Gabrielle von Rosenberg". Sabato finds her in "un Gotha" (*A*, 76). The Rosenberg family is indeed in the *Almanaque de Gotha* but, of course, Hedwig is not. The reason for choosing that particular surname is also connected with Nazi Germany: Hedwig is said to be the daughter of a general in Hitler's Wehrmacht and has the same name—although she is not related to him—as the author of *The Myth of the Twentieth Century*, Alfred Rosenberg, a prominent figure in Nazi Germany whose philosophy, tinged with occultism, was influential in the formation of Nazi "mythology".[33]

Schneider's persecution of Sabato is connected with Germany in ways more significant than in the use of the same names. The presence in Buenos Aires of Schneider and Hedwig and the memory of Molinelli's assertion that

Hitler was the Antichrist led Sabato to study "lo que pudiera sobre logias y sectas secretas bajo el régimen nazi" (A, 79). What he studied was, once more, Le Matin des magiciens, although he does not say so. The curious account about Hitler in the novel (A, 70-83) is taken in every detail from that book (pp. 433-443). According to Sabato and Pauwels and Bergier, satanic power was vested in Karl Haushofer, the geopolitician and close friend of Rudolf Hess. Haushofer was supposed to have been a prominent member of the Left Hand Sect and other occult societies that flourished during the Third Reich.³⁴ It was he who, through Hess, recruited Hitler "cuando todavía era un cabito" (A, 80) and turned him into what he became. Sabato concludes: "me inclino a creer que Haushofer era de verdad un instrumento del Demonio y que Hitler era su médium" (A, 82).³⁵ This is the sort of relationship, as will be remembered, that he assumed existed between Schneider and Hedwig and which increases his danger, for "el ocultismo nos enseña que luego de haberse atraído las potencias del Mal, los miembros del grupo pueden actuar mediante un Mago, que a su vez lo hace a través de un médium" (A, 82).³⁶ As we see, historical and private events are interpreted in the same way because they are both part of a single problem, the problem of evil. As Bruno said at the beginning, and as I have quoted above, what happened to these people is "lo que puede suceder con la humanidad toda".

Haushofer's supposed membership of the Left Hand Sect (the left is the feminine and evil side) gave Sabato the opportunity to add another dimension to his concern about nuclear physics. It was the members of this sect who, according to Sabato and Pauwels and Bergier, caused the total destruction of an ancient and flourishing civilisation in what is now the Gobi Desert, by means of an atomic explosion.³⁷ Scientists today have not learned the lesson of this legend: "(y las leyendas como los mitos tienen siempre algo verdadero o significativo)" (A, 80). Newton may have known about nuclear fission and withheld his knowledge; Sabato quotes Newton as saying: "Esta manera de impregnar el mercurio fue mantenida en secreto por los que sabían y constituye probablemente el pórtico de algo más noble [que la fabricación del oro], algo que no puede ser comunicado sin que el mundo corra un inmenso peligro" (A, 295). Sabato takes this quotation from Le Matin too.³⁸ The historical dimensions of Sabato's predicament thus extend far and wide.

I would not be true to the spirit of the novel if I were to omit a reference to the note of hope that it contains. It also belongs to those episodes in the historical path being dealt with at this point. This note of hope is negative, ambiguous, and unemphatic. It is placed in the body of the novel, not at the beginning nor, particularly, the end. This is significantly different from Sobre héroes y tumbas, where the hopeful departure of Martín for Patagonia occupies the final page. It is negative in the sense that Nacho's hope for a better future results (like Martín's) from his failure to commit suicide, rather than from anything positive. It is ambiguous, in the sense that very little, if anything, is promised to the departing Nacho, even less than was promised to Martín. But Nacho's plot does not really belong here, since his is a personal problem. Marcelo, however, is indirectly involved in Che Guevara's political struggle. Marcelo harbours a companion of Guevara, Palito, who has taken refuge in Buenos Aires. In a long section (pp. 249-268), Palito relates Che Guevara's last struggle in Bolivia, his capture and his death. Marcelo, Guevara and Palito are presented in the most flattering light possible. Marcelo is without a blemish: Sabato, "delante de él se sentía siempre culpable [. . .] por su bondad, por su callada reserva, por su delicadeza" (A, 186). Palito, like Carlos, whose spirit he "repeats", is "un espíritu puro y religioso" (SHT, 412). As for Guevara, one can only feel admiration (A, 204). We must remember, though, that Marcelo dies after suffering horrific tortures (described with those of others in the most gory detail, pp. 474-489) and that Palito will no doubt undergo a similar fate. Their sacrifice is estimated by Bruno in purely idealistic, romantic terms: it is "un absoluto, la dignidad del hombre se salvó una vez más con su solo acto" (A, 205). Their martyrdom is merely exemplary and is recorded in the novel in the hope that it will not be wasted "en el tumulto y el caos, sino que pueda alcanzar el corazón de otros hombres, para removerlos y salvarlos" (A, 17) in spirit only. The revolution, too, is equally futile in practice: "Este sacrificio sería inútil y candoroso, porque el nuevo orden sería copado por cínicos o negociantes" (A, 204). Such also was the fate of the Russian Revolution: "también había sido romántica, poetas la habían cantado. Porque toda revolución, por pura que sea, y sobre todo si lo es, está destinada a convertirse en una sucia y policial burocracia, mientras los mejores espíritus concluyen en las mazmorras o en los manicomios" (A, 204).

At the key position of the novel, the end, Bruno once more reflects on these matters. He fails to indicate how any promise of hope could ever be fulfilled. Frustration and a "perpetuo desencuentro" are the "inevitable destino de todo ser que ha nacido para morir", including "el revolucionario puro ante la triste materialización de aquellos ideales que años antes defendió con su sufrimiento en medio de atroces torturas" (A, 527). Readers may well wonder if the immortality of fiction, or even history, promised by the novel is sufficient inducement for men to give up their lives. Even in the phrase used by Bruno, "no hay felicidad absoluta", the "absoluta" is but a rhetorical concession, for there is no single case of even "relative" happiness in Abaddón. Like the Gnostic Basilides, he seems to think that "l'angoisse et la misère accompagnent l'existence comme la rouille couvre le fer".[39]

"En toda gran novela, en toda gran tragedia, hay una cosmovisión inmanente," Sabato asserts in El escritor y sus fantasmas (p. 262). The episodes included in Abaddón that are connected with recent history are there in order to demonstrate the "truth" of his cosmovisión. Even the "pure spirits" like Marcelo and Palito cannot escape the fate that Evil has decreed for all men. All they can hope to achieve by their generous actions is *not* to contribute to the general evil in the world.

★   ★   ★

If we turn now to what I previously called "the private path" and follow Sabato's life, we shall see how important is the part played by sex and by psychic powers. Looking back on his life, Sabato can now uncover the path it is following towards knowledge and emancipation: he can distinguish a "plot"; "desde aquella época," he says, "he tratado de descifrar la trama secreta. . . En estos últimos tiempos, no obstante, he intentado atar cabos sueltos que parecen orientarme en el laberinto" (*A*, 338). However, that knowledge can only be gained, not rationally, but by means of direct participation in evil.

Sabato suffered from somnambulism until he was thirteen. Carlos' sleep-walking experiences as a child in "La fuente muda" have a basis in his own life.[40] He says in *Abaddón*: "El sonambulismo. Adónde iba cuando me levantaba de niño? Qué continentes había recorrido en aquellos viajes? Mi cuerpo iba a la sala al cuarto de mis padres. Pero mi alma? El cuerpo se mueve por un lado o permanence en su cama, pero el alma divaga por ahí" (*A*, 338). He makes the body and soul change places. Having inferred that the soul stays behind while the body leaves its bed, he concludes that the reverse must also be true—that while the body is asleep, the soul will roam free. Premonitions provide evidence for this conclusion. The soul's faculty for moving outside the body means, too, outside time and space. The soul can thus witness future events and bring back the "knowledge".

The Sabato of the novel discovered very early in life that he had the gift of foresight. One day, while still at school in Rojas in 1923, he found himself "corriendo hacia la casa de los Etchebarne" (*A*, 315). María Etche-barne was a teacher with whom he was in love. When he arrived at the house, he found her writhing in agony on the floor: someone had thrown acid into her eyes and blinded her. The premonition that something was going to happen and the horror of the scene the child actually witnessed must have remained deeply ingrained in his mind. But the most important thing in this episode is that Sabato's first experience of love is "linked" with evil, and with eyes. The child, if I am right, established an irrational line of causality between love and blindness. Furthermore, foreknowledge of the event was possible *without the use of sight*, thus establishing another link between blindness and knowledge. An important irrational cluster of relations between love, blindness and knowledge is thus created at a critical point for the young Sabato.[41] The lasting importance of this episode is brought out by its "repetition" in Paris fifteen years later, in 1938. Travelling one day on the underground, he notices a woman who *has* María Etchbarne's eyes. This incident, as we shall see, is also connected with the account of one of his *desdoblamientos*.[42] This is what happened in Paris. Determined to find the woman with María's eyes, he returns to the underground station where he saw her and keeps watch on the trains for many hours and days. The watch proves pointless, but one day, at the Church of St Eustace, where he is attending a concert, he feels that her eyes are again fixed on the back of his neck (*A*, 318). At the end of the concert, he follows the possessor of the eyes to a building in the rue Montsouris but then, not knowing what to do, he is content to go and sit in a café. While he is there, he suddenly feels compelled (as he did as a child in Rojas) to run back to the woman's house. Unerringly, he finds her flat, and when he goes in, finds her with "sus manos apretadas como garras sobre su cara, sin dejar de gemir del mismo modo que ciertos animales moribundos" (*A*, 319-320). All he can do, knowing exactly what has happened, is to return to his lodgings. When next day he relates these events to a friend, Bonasso, he is told that he could not have gone to the concert in St Eustace nor to the woman's flat since he was with Bonasso and others all the evening. The vividness of his experience encourages him to check both his friends' assertions and the events of the rue Montsouris. Both prove to be accurate. A certain Madame Verrier, who lived in the flat visited by Sabato the previous night, did have a terrible accident, and was in hospital. Sabato had actually been in two places at once, "aunque hubiese sido en sueños" (*A*, 321), he is forced to conclude.

It would, I think, be pointless to determine, even if it were possible, whether such experiences as the one described above did or did not happen to Sabato "in real life". His firm and unequivocal attribution of a cognitive function to literature, the seriousness with which he approaches his task as a writer, his repeated dismissal of formal innovations in literature, together with his belief in the significance of dreams and hallucinations, demand that we should consider his creative activity on a par with psychic experiences. Furthermore, Sabato considers the task of character invention as a *desoblamiento* in the sense of Astral Projection and not because "los personajes profundos de una novela salen siempre del propio creador" (*EF*, 91), as is probably the case for most novelists. Man is dual, he has a "doble condición de sapo y ángel" (*EF*, 157), and Sabato finds it confirmed by such phenomena as somnabulism and premonitions, to which—as we saw—he has been subject.[43]

About Fernando Vidal, he said: "creo que representa mi parte peor, mi lado nocturno" (*EF*, 22). Sabato has not concealed his *lado nocturno* under another name in *Abaddón*, but he has split it into two: himself and R. This character is responsible for encouraging Sabato's baser instincts, but it is Sabato that carries out R.'s ideas. The plan for blinding a sparrow was attributed to Fernando (as well as its execution) in *Sobre héroes y tumbas* (p. 391); Bruno was then a horrified witness. The incident is retold here, but it is Sabato who carries out the mutilation under the instigation of R.

R. is responsible, too, for the temporary breakdown of his marriage: "Por entonces yo me había ido a vivir solo, abandonando a M. y a mi hijo, de la manera más despiadada" (A, 317). We know this separation to be a fact.[44] With a candour that does him credit, he does not gloss over the worst aspects of his life; the novel bears, in this respect, a telling epigraph from Lermontov's *A Hero of our Time*: "Es posible que mañana muera, y en la tierra no quedará nadie que me haya conocido por completo. Unos me considerarán peor pero otros mejor de lo que soy. Algunos dirán que era una buena persona; otros que era un canalla. Pero las dos opiniones serán igualmente equivocadas".[45] This is an obvious plea for indulgence for Sabato's tragically split personality.

As I said, I think that the María Etchebarne episode is of vital importance for the understanding of subsequent events, particularly the Soledad incident. In the latter, we are left in no doubt that love, or more specifically, the sexual act, leads to "blindness". "En lugar del sexo Soledad tenía un enorme ojo grisverdoso que lo observaba con sombría expectiva, con dura ansiedad" (A, 468), which Sabato is forced to pierce in a "monstruoso rito" (A, 463).[46] The belief that matter is evil is central to Gnostic thought, as I pointed out earlier; but one does not need to turn to Gnostic thought, which considers that *all* matter is evil, to find sex associated with sin and corruption. "We are born between faeces and urine," said St Augustine.[47] The Fall is inextricably mixed with sinful sex, hence the importance of the purity of the Virgin Mary in the Catholic cult. Before the "monstruoso rito" is performed, R. draws their attention (and ours) to the place where it is about to take place: "Estamos bajo la cripta de la iglesia de Belgrano. La conocés. Esa iglesia redonda. La iglesia de la Inmaculada Concepción—agregó con tono irónico" (A, 467). Several characters in this and earlier novels have had a less than immaculate conception. On Mothers' Day, Nacho sends his mother, to whom he refers as a whore, a condom (A, 110), and Ledesma, another Gnostic who expresses his antinomian feelings by "streaking", and who is the author of four *comunicaciones* setting out "por qué y para qué fuimos fabricados" (A, 114), says he was born "cuando ya mi padre ya no podía ver a mi madre"; he adds that poets, instead of singing "al crepúsculo", should really sing "al crepus-culo" (A, 183). There are too many well-known references in Sabato's earlier fiction to this sort of thing to list them here. It is a typically Gnostic belief. The Gnostic's feelings are made "avant tout de répugnance, à l'endroit des principaux événements de notre vie charnelle (conception, naissance, maladies, mort, etc.) et, singulièrement, des diverses manifestations de la sexualité."[48] Woman is also the "matter" and "mater" of the alchemists as Fulcanelli explains.[49] If all matter is evil, sex will be doubly so, since it is precisely the way that matter is created, and hence the means by which evil is propagated. This sort of thinking can lead to the existence of two apparently contradictory moralities: complete asceticism and absolute libertinism.[50] The former is understandable, but it is more difficult to see the type of reasoning behind the paradox of the latter, and it is the latter that, in a sense, we find represented in Sabato. Moral law, or so antinomian libertinism would have it, is as much part of the evil tyranny imposed by Satan as anything else. Hence, freedom from the moral yoke is also a means of escaping demonic domination: "No es que todo esté permitido. Estamos *obligados* a hacer todo," says Agustina (*A*, 456).[51]

This will help us to understand the paradox implied in Sabato's novel: that sex is evil, but figures prominently in Sabato's struggle *against* evil. "El hombre es un ser dual—dijo Sabato—. Tragicamente dual. Y lo grave, lo estúpido es que desde Sócrates se ha querido proscribir su lado oscuro" (*A*, 285). Sabato goes beyond the mere avoidance of his *lado oscuro*: he actively encourages it in order to free himself from Schneider and the *Entidad*, that is to say, Satan. This is the type of argument, I think, which underlies the Soledad episode and the other "love" episodes presently to be discussed.

Soledad is treated very differently from most of the rest of the characters in *Abaddón*. Very little is done to disguise the symbolic significance she is intended to have. But the symbolism is unusual in the sense that, in addition to the meaning I have been suggesting—a metaphysical dimension to sex,— she bears a special relationship to some other female characters. She is not herself an individual: she is part of others, in the same way, though perhaps less obviously, as R. is a part of Sabato. Whose part she is will become clear when Agustina and *la mujer de LA TENAZA* are discussed. The creatures, as well as their creator, are split. I said that very little is done to disguise her symbolic role. She remains silent throughout; Sabato feels her presence, knows she is there *before* he sees her. We are quite familiar with this form of telepathic communication from earlier fiction, and elsewhere in *Abaddón*. When Soledad first appears, in 1927, it is in a house in La Plata which belongs to Nicolás Ortiz de Rozas, and in a room where a portrait of Juan Manuel de Rosas hangs on the wall: "El Tirano Sangriento me contemplaba (no, el verbo adecuado es me 'observaba')", explains Sabato, "desde la eternidad con su mirada helada y gris, con su boca apretada sin labios" (*A*, 301). The homonyms Rosas and Rozas and Soledad's likeness to the old dictator constitute three ominous synchronic links. And the links *are* synchronic because she is not related to either.

However, this form of "reincarnation", or *desdoblamiento* in time, is another feature of Sabato's fiction—or I should say, rather, of his metaphysics —with which we are also familiar. I am not, of course, referring to the old Balzacian or Galdosian reappearance of characters in subsequent novels. This happens in *Abaddón* too, where we re-encounter Castel, Martín, etc. What I mean is the sort of thing I had in mind when I said at the beginning that Fernando was now Sabato and Alejandra, Agustina. And it goes beyond the simple repetition of old material. These characters are archetypal or have archetypal functions, and their reappearance represents a reappearance of the symbolic import they have in Sabato's thought, which *is* constant.

There is a shuffling of identities during the sleepless night he spends "dreaming" before the second meeting with *la mujer de LA TENAZA*: "Calsen se convertía en Costa, la pobre chica de barrio [first, Dora Forte (*A*, 36), then Alejandra (*A*, 38)] *en la mujer de LA TENAZA, hermana y amante* de Costa" (*A*, 416). We will return later to this clue. Palito, the *guerrillero* protected by Marcelo, reincarnates Carlos: "¿No estaba de nuevo [Carlos] al lado de Marcelo? Porque los espíritus se repiten, casi encarnado en la misma cara ardiente de aquel Carlos de 1932" (*A*, 193). This is the Carlos of "La fuente muda", who also appears, as I said, in *Sobre héroes y tumbas*,[52] and in whom Sabato has put again so much of himself. The reincarnation of Rosas in Soledad is obviously not quite the same, because Rosas has never appeared in Sabato's fiction, at least not "openly". There were hints at his archetypal nature in the previous novel, hints that he was the "dark side" of the nation because, in a family of "unitarians", "ni Fernando ni yo lo somos," says Alejandra (*SHT*, 45). Referring to Rosas as Soledad's *antepasado* is more than a hint that we are to see in Soledad the embodiment of primeval forces also embodied in Rosas—not, of course, a specific historic character. This sort of regression to one of the contraries forming the *unidad primigenia* is the recommended task of the artist—to return to "las regiones inmemoriales de la raza, allí donde dominan los instintos básicos de la vida y de la muerte, donde el sexo y el incesto, la paternidad y el parricidio, mueven sus fantasmas" (*EF*, 263).

This quotation leads us to a topic of great importance—incest,—but I must postpone discussing this until I have dealt with some other characteristics of Soledad and her "complementary" characters. These other characteristics are, in fact, the most obvious pointers to her symbolic function. She moves "con una sensualidad parecida a la que tienen las víboras" (*A*, 308). She gives the impression of violence held in check "como en una caldera. Pero una caldera alimentada con fuego helado" (*A*, 307), hinting at both Eve and Laura as her ancestors. This is one reason why her age, too, is so extraordinary: she is fifteen, yet "ahora me digo que podría tener mil y haber vivido en tiempos remotísimos" (*A*, 303)—an obvious pointer, if ever there was one, to her significance.[53] "Su nombre correspondía a lo que era: parecía guardar un sagrado secreto de esos que deben guardar bajo juramento los miembros de ciertas sectas" (*A*, 307). The meeting between Soledad and Sabato for the "monstruoso rito" (*A*, 463) does not take place in La Plata in the house of Nicolás Ortiz de Rozas, but in the house of the Carranzas, who lived in the calle de Arcos in 1927. The steps that led Sabato to the house are carefully and accurately described and it is possible to follow them on a map of Buenos Aires.[54] The house in the calle de Arcos is not far from the Church of Belgrano, under which the *rito* takes place. But when Sabato returns in 1972, as he had been told in Paris in 1938 that he would have to do ("hay que tener el coraje del retorno," R. has said to him), and goes down into the underground passages of the house, nothing is said of what happens there. He goes down "porque algo le estaba esperando. Pero no sabía qué" (*A*, 470). The reader is not told either. Immediately after his descent, the arduous ascent starts, through slime, rats and other infernal animals. Sabato emerges in the morning into the teeming city of Buenos Aires, unseen, unheard, unnoticed by the millions going to work. When he arrives home, we are told: "entró en su estudio. Delante de la mesa de trabajo estaba Sabato sentado" (*A*, 473). As in Paris earlier, only his soul had gone to the calle de Arcos, but unlike Paris, we are left to puzzle over what happened to this part of him.

Just as in *Sobre héroes y tumbas*, we are left in the dark as to the nature of a crucial appointment. But I do not think that there is real ambiguity in either novel. In both cases, careful reading reveals the clues to the mystery.[55] The sequence of events leading to Sabato's return to the now deserted house in the calle de Arcos and its underground passages is complicated by the fact that the sequence of the sections in the novel does not always correspond to it. But it is not impossible to reconstruct it. The mysterious woman he meets in the café LA TENAZA has all the characteristics previously attributed to Soledad: extreme youth and extreme age, the sensuousness of a snake and the power of telepathic communication. She is in LA TENAZA reading LOS OJOS Y LA VIDA SEXUAL, with a cover illustration by Leonor Fini (*A*, 415). Sabato is profoundly disturbed, "como ausente, como quien está fascinado por algo que lo aísla de la realidad", the condition we have seen described earlier as being in a "pozo". Sabato does not even acknowledge Bruno's arrival; all he can do is to watch the "serpientegato prehistórico" lying in wait for him, held spellbound by her "radiaciones". Eventually, though, he does leave the café. He returns the following day, sure of finding her there; when he is able to overcome his fear, he goes up to her, saying simply: "Ya estoy aquí" (*A*, 417). Like Soledad, she never speaks (though we know the character of her voice), and she disappears from the novel after this meeting, except for the mention of an appointment with her (*A*, 448); this appointment is to take place in the calle Crámer, where Sabato also has a meeting with someone called Nora, never before—or afterwards—mentioned in the novel. These two things together seem to suggest strongly that *la mujer de LA TENAZA* and Nora are one and the same person. This, however, is not of great importance, since we do not know who Nora is. What matters is her ultimate identity. In this respect there are some curious clues. When Sabato arrives in the calle Crámer, "le pareció ver la fugitiva sombra de Agustina" (*A*, 448). Now the calle Crámer and calle de Arcos are but a few steps from each other and are both in Belgrano, near the round church that we already know so well. We shall see presently the importance of the location of these two streets. With the meeting with *la mujer de LA TENAZA* "comenzó el hundimiento en una ciénaga fosforescente"; Sabato feels that through her begins "una lenta y complicada corrupción", which would entail "el sacrificio de Agustina" (*A*, 417). We are not told how this could be so, nor what sort of sacrifice it is. We know from the beginning of the novel that she consented to a degrading affaire with Pérez Nassif, her employer, and that this leads to the breakdown, towards the end of the novel, of her (in all likelihood) incestuous relationship with her brother Nacho. But how could Sabato's meeting with Nora, or *la mujer de LA TENAZA*, affect Agustina's relationship with her brother, if indeed this does constitute her "sacrifice"? If we consider Agustina's relationship with Sabato, an answer suggests itself and a connection, not synchronistic but simply causal, is found.

Agustina has a final stormy meeting with Sabato which occupies a very short section (9 lines of varying length, but not strictly speaking a poem), couched in poetic, metaphorical language (*A*, 453). Sabato says beforehand: "cuando estuvieron juntos sintió el abismo que se había abierto entre los dos". Then, Agustina "se convirtió en una llamante furia", hurling insults at him, tearing his mind with her claws—Alejandra without the gun. Symbolically, her reaction reflects her duality, the duality of an *ángel exterminador*, but on the narrative plane we do not know what has brought it about. As I said, it takes place after the meeting in the calle Crámer where Agustina saw Sabato with Nora, and I think that there is an element of jealousy in Agustina's behaviour; but Sabato's reaction is not that of a "betraying lover". Explaining the episode as a case of simple jealousy trivialises it in this context. What the incident certainly demonstrates quite clearly is that between Sabato and Agustina there has been more than simple acquaintance. It is also clear that Sabato will not be the only one to suffer. Sabato's meeting with Nora does then lead to the "sacrifice" of Agustina, and this scene expresses it.

The early stages of Sabato and Agustina's relationship do suggest that a strong mutual attraction is felt by both from the start. When Nacho angrily reproaches Sabato for the frivolous vanity and social ambition that he shows in his professional life, she alone follows him outside LA BIELA, where the incident takes place, to apologise on behalf of her brother. From that moment, a bond is established. At their next meeting, "los dos sabían que el encuentro era inevitable". But the most significant clue as to what did pass between them is an isolated short section (*A*, 163) describing a meeting between Sabato and Agustina in Belgrano *in the square in front of the round church of the Immaculate Conception*. Nacho, who has followed his sister, no doubt jealously suspicious of her activities (and here we must remember his parallel action which led to the discovery of her affaire with Pérez Nassif), sees her "a la luz del farol, concentrada, mirando ya al suelo ya a sus costados. Fue entonces cuando vio acercarse a Sabato. Ella se levantó rapidamente y él la tomó del brazo con decisión y se fueron *hacia el lado de la calle Arcos*, por Echeverría" (*A*, 163). Nothing more is said about Agustina and Sabato until Sabato's meeting with *la mujer de LA TENAZA* in the calle Crámer, some 200 pages later, but the importance of this episode cannot be over-stressed. A similar number of pages separates the moment when Martín, who has also followed Alejandra to the same spot in Belgrano, sees her entering the house whose underground passages also lead to the crypt of the Immaculate Conception, and the identification, at the end of the "Informe", of the woman that Fernando meets in that same house. This meeting is the only indication in the novel that the "algo que le estaba esperando" when he returns to the underground passages of the calle de Arcos, and about which we are told nothing, is in fact a meeting with Agustina. The dream that I quoted earlier, in which Sabato shuffles the identities of characters, was another clue. In it, "la pobre chica de barrio" became *la mujer de LA TENAZA*, "hermana y amante" of Nacho, not of Costa, as we were told in the "dream".[56]

I think it can all be traced to the María Etchebarne episode at school. I suggested that the Soledad affair was a symbolic re-enactment of the childish love that had led to blindness. Then we saw how through a *desdoblamiento*, Sabato relived in Paris the Etchebarne incident. I suggest now that through another *desdoblamiento*, Sabato is reliving his relationship with Agustina, a relationship which is "against nature" and therefore leads to her sacrifice and the final tragic confluence of all the plots. For *la mujer de LA TENAZA* whom he meets when she is reading LOS OJOS Y LA VIDA SEXUAL is Agustina, or a part of Agustina, as Soledad was María Etchebarne.

I said "against nature" because the relationship between Agustina and Sabato must, I think, be considered incestuous. I say this for the most obvious reason that Agustina is the creature of his imagination. However, there is a difference between *Abaddón* and any other novel peopled by the author's creatures which justifies my assertion. Sabato is *inside* his own fiction, and he makes great play of this. In their first meeting, Agustina says to him: "Señor Sabato—su voz era trémula—, quiero decir . . . mi hermano y yo . . . sus personajes . . . digo, Castel, Alejandra . . ." (*A*, 66). He is inside the novel in more senses than the presence of a character called Sabato indicates, because his characters are his own *desdoblamientos*. Not only are R. and Bruno obvious projections of himself, but Nacho too, that part of himself that refuses to compromise. He lives with his fictional characters as he lives with "real" people—his wife, his children and friends.[57] However, this is for Sabato much more than a literary device: it is a significant activity leading, because literature is a form of knowledge, to the discovery of the Truth. Through the creation of and involvement with fictional characters, among whom he himself is not the least important, Sabato immerses himself in the primeval forces of evil that shaped the world "donde el sexo y el incesto, la paternidad y el parricidio mueven sus fantasmas" (*EF*, 263). His women are archetypal, symbolic figures who suggest these forces, which are inside him as much as outside him. Like the alchemist attempting the transmutation of metals, his aim is his own transformation. The horrible transformation of his "double" into a bat is the final stage in his progression. He has achieved through the instrument of Agustina full knowledge, the Gnosis he set out to discover.[58]

It will be seen that we have come full circle. In the final sections of the novel, Sabato's and Nacho's paths synchronically converge. Nacho refuses to compromise and, undressing Agustina, completes her degradation by spitting on her sex. Marcelo dies a brutal death, and Sabato's "double" undergoes a horrible transformation and becomes a bat. "A esa misma hora los reyes magos están en camino." All plots converge at Epiphany, on the 6th of January, when a star guided the Magi to Bethlehem; a star has guided Sabato, too, to his Epiphany: the six-pointed star which, according to Fulcanelli, "rayonne sur la face du compost, c'est à dire au dessus de la crèche de l'enfant Jésus",[59] and which is the hermetic star, "le signe caractéristique de l'œuvre, la seule étoile".[60] The Virgin to whom Sabato has been led in the crypt of the Immaculate Conception is Isis, the incestuous mother of all things. Sabato has followed, it seems, Fulcanelli's advice:

> Et maintenant, travaillez de jour si bon vous semble; mais ne nous accusez pas si vos efforts n'aboutissent jamais qu'à l'insuccès. Nous savons, quant à nous, que la déesse Isis est la mère de toutes choses, qu'elle les porte toutes dans son sein, et qu'elle seule est la dispensatrice de la *Révélation* et de l'*Initiation*. Profanes qui avez des yeux pour ne point voir et des oreilles pour ne point entendre, à qui adresserez-vous donc vos prières? Ignorez-vous qu'on ne parvient à Jésus que par l'intercession de sa *Mère; sancta Maria ora pro nobis*? Et la Vierge est figurée, pour votre instruction, les pieds posés sur le croissant lunaire, toujours vêtue de bleu, couleur symbolique de l'astre des nuits. Nous pourrions dire beaucoup plus, mais nous avons assez parlé.
>
> (*Le Mystère des cathédrales*, p. 174).

After the climax of the novel, which culminates in Sabato's transformation into a bat, there is a sort of Epilogue (pp. 500-528), in which Bruno recounts the death of his father in 1953,[61] and a journey twenty years later in 1973 to Capitán Olmos—the fictional Rojas—and its cemetery. There he finds the tomb of Sabato—the fictional Sabato—on whose gravestone we read the request that a single word should follow his name: *paz*. This word must again, I think, be understood in Gnostic terms as the final emancipation from the world, the final knowledge of himself, of the spiritual being finally released. As Puech puts it, "posé sur le plan de devenir, le problème sotériologique se dissout en se résolvant en fonction d'une ontologie."[62] This is why, instead of sadness, Bruno Bassán considers "como amistoso imaginarlo muerto y enterrado" (*A*, 526). His reflections, after that, dissolve into a final poem which laments the fate of the soul in the world, guided by "la voz *lunar* de la *hermana* [. . .] de *tempestuosa* tristeza" (*A*, 528): what Agustina, symbolically, had been for Sabato.

There is little doubt in my mind that Sabato takes his calling as an artist with the utmost seriousness. I think that he would want his novel to be read as a "revelation", not needing my interpretation nor that of any other critic, but directly, as he says, as an "ontofanía y punto".

St Andrews

SALVADOR BACARISSE

NOTES

[1] Buenos Aires: Editorial Sudamericana, 1974. References are to this edition, and are given in the text with the title abbreviated: *A*, followed by the page number. Other editions and abbreviations used are as follows: *El túnel*, Buenos Aires: Editorial Sudamericana (Col. Piragua), 1972: *T*. *Sobre héroes y tumbas*, Buenos Aires: Editorial Sudamericana (Col. Piragua), 1972: *SHT*. *El escritor y sus fantasmas*, Buenos Aires: Aguilar Argentina, 1971: *EF*. *Hombres y engranajes. Heterodoxia*, (one vol.), Madrid: Alianza Editorial (Libro de bolsillo), 1973: *HE,H*. *Uno y el universo*, Buenos Aires: Editorial Sudamericana (Col. Índice), 1975: *U*.

[2] So spelt, without the accent, in *Abaddón* and since its publication, presumably because of the unpleasant associations the name has with "Saturno, Ángel de la Soledad en la Cábala, Espíritu del Mal para ciertos ocultistas, el Sabbath de los hechiceros (*A*, 23). "Anotaciones para 'El escritor en la catástrofe' ", *Nueva narrativa hispanoamericana*, IV, 1974, 7-15, is still by Sábato, but not the *Diálogos* with Borges quoted below, note 11.

[3] As Frank Kermode, *The Sense of an Ending*, New York, 1967, demonstrates with examples taken from literature in English.

[4] Mircea Eliade, "Cultural Fashions and History of Religions", in *Occultism, Witchcraft and Cultural Fashions*, Chicago, 1976, p. 8. Colin Wilson speaks of the "occult boom" and makes it start with *Le Matin des magiciens*. See Colin Wilson, *Strange Powers*, London, 1975, p. 15.

[5] I shall henceforth refer to this book by its shorter title, followed by a page number where applicable.

[6] *Sur*, XVI (1947), 24-63. Much of this story is, no doubt, autobiographical: "Yo me uní a los terroristas . . . [Sabato says] de forma que en mí la rebelión asumió la forma más violenta . . . casi de violencia física". Walter Mauro, Elena Clementelli (editors), *Los escritores frente al poder*, Barcelona, 1975, p. 212.

[7] Nelly Martínez, "Fernando Vidal Olmos y el Surrealismo: una conversación con Ernesto Sábato" [on 28 August, 1971], *Sin nombre*, 2-3 (1972), 61.

[8] In an interview with Emir Rodríguez Monegal and Severo Sarduy, he stated this opinion once more: "Creo que un escritor tiene una sola obsesión que expresar en su obra. A tumbos un poco, a través de su vida, en borradores probablemente cada vez menos imperfectos, toda su vida intenta encarnizadamente ahondar en ese secreto de su propia existencia . . . Yo siento que estoy siempre hablando de lo mismo". Ernesto Sábato, "Por una novela novelesca y metafísica", *Mundo nuevo*, No. 5, 1966, 15. Reprinted in Emir Rodríguez Monegal. *El arte de narrar*, 2nd ed., Caracas, s.d., p. 240.

[9] Joaquín Neyra. *Ernesto Sábato*. Buenos Aires, 1973, p. 54.

[10] Quoted by James Olney, *Metaphors of Self*, Princeton, 1972, p. 4.

[11] J. L. Borges y E. Sabato, *Diálogos*, Buenos Aires, 1976, p. 169.

[12] Ibid. My italics.

[13] Op. cit., p. 196.

[14] Op. cit., p. 149.

[15] Op. cit., p. 148.

[16] "Una teoría sobre la predicción del porvenir" in *Las ciencias ocultas*, Buenos Aires, 1967, pp. 137-154 and Sabato's interview with César Tiempo, "Ernesto Sábato . . . habla sobre el Sueño, la Ficción y la Eternidad", *Estafeta literaria*, No. 370 (Madrid, 2.5.1967), 14-15. (This reproduces "Sábato habla sobre el infierno, las premoniciones y la eternidad", *El tiempo* [Bogotá, 5.2.1967], "Suplemento semanal", pp. 1-2.)

[17] See the "Interrogatorio preliminar" in *EF*; Ángela B. Dellepiane, *Ernesto Sábato. El escritor y la obra*, New York, 1968; Harley Dean Oberhelman, *Ernesto Sábato*, New York, 1970; María Angélica Correa, *Genio y figura de Ernesto Sábato*, Buenos Aires, 1971 and Joaquín Neyra, op. cit.

[18] See for example, from a vast literature, Colin Wilson, *The Occult*, London, 1973, p. 59 ff; Fulcanelli, *Le Mystère des cathédrales*, Paris, 1964, p. 57; *Le Matin*, p. 318 and Arthur Koestler, *The Roots of Coincidence*, London, 1974.

[19] There are many references to the absence of chance in his writings, and in the interview with Rodríguez Monegal and Sarduy quoted above he said: "En la novela [*SHT*] se dice muy a menudo que no hay casualidades sino causalidades y finalidades en la vida de los hombres. Lo creo profundamente". (*Mundo nuevo*, No. 5, 1968, 17).

[20] C. G. Jung, "Synchronicity: an acausal connecting principle", in *The Structure and Dynamics of the Psyche. Collected Works*, Vol. 8, London, 1960, pp. 417-519, esp. paras. 849, 856 and 858. A discussion of the principle is found in Arthur Koestler, op. cit. pp. 82-105.

[21] "Porque siempre caminamos con un rumbo fijo, en ocasiones determinado por nuestra voluntad más visible, pero en otras, quizá más decisivas para nuestra existencia, por una voluntad desconocida aun para nosotros mismos, pero no obstante poderosa e inmanejable . . ." (*A*, 432-3). Another "cause" is suggested in *SHT*: the unformulated wish of a person. So it is that Fernando "causes" Iglesias' accident without his physical intervention (*SHT*, Part III, Ch. 7).

[22] Op. cit., para. 856.

[23] Barragán had already had an Apocalyptic vision in *SHT*: "el mundo tiene que ser purgado con sangre y fuego . . ." (p. 190).

[24] In another place in the novel, the simultaneous presence of three people in a café is referred to as a "triángulo cabalístico" (*A*, 450).

[25] Philo (c. 30 B.C. - A.D. 50), *De Oficio Mundi*, Vol. I, London, 1929, p. 13 f. Quoted by Christopher Butler, *Number Symbolism*, London, 1970, pp. 22-3.

[26] Sabato holds that literature has a cognitive function, that the writer should not be guided by aesthetic or formal considerations: "La literatura ha adquirido una nueva dignidad a la que no estaba acostumbrada: la del conocimiento" (*EF*, 84). Also *EF*, 87-89, 91, 142-3, 157-8, etc., and "Una teoría sobre la predicción del porvenir", op. cit., p. 149.

[27] Charles-Henri Puech, "Phénoménologie de la Gnose" in *En Quête de la Gnose*, Paris, 1978, I, 201. Since there are many Gnostic sects, sometimes holding conflicting beliefs, the Gnostic religion as a whole can only be a "synthesis". However, the belief in the evil origin of the world is, according to Hans Jonas, and other authorities, a central one: "The cardinal feature of Gnostic thought is the radical dualism that governs the relation of God and the world, and correspondingly that of man and the world. The deity is absolutely transmundane, its nature alien to that of the universe, which it neither created nor governs and to which it is the complete antithesis: to the divine realm of light, self-contained and remote, the cosmos is opposed as the realm of darkness". (Hans Jonas, *The Gnostic Religion*, Beacon Hill, Boston, 1958, p. 42). The "antijudaism" expressed by Sabato is also typical. "The ultimate Jewish origin of the Mandaeans or Nasōraean sect cannot . . . be denied, although there are vehement polemics against the Jews in the Mandaean literature. Moses is held to be a false prophet and the Jewish god Adōnai an evil god or demon". Kurt Rudolph, *Mandaeism*, Leiden, 1978, p. 4. See also C.-H. Puech, "Où en est le problème du gnosticisme?" op. cit., I, 152-3. This does not imply antisemitism on the part of Sabato. He has been most outspoken about the injustice of harbouring Nazi criminals in Argentina. See "Documentos" in Neyra, op. cit., pp. 129-133.

[28] See note 17.

[29] Fulcanelli, whose real name is still unknown, is the author of two remarkable books: *Le Mystère des cathédrales*, Paris: J. Schemit, 1926, and *Les Demeures philosophales*, Paris: J. Schemit, 1930, which interpret the hermetic significance of emblematic figures in monuments throughout France. Both books have been reprinted; Paris: Jean Jacques Pauvert, 1964. All page references are to the 1964 edition. Fulcanelli is also mentioned in Cortázar, *Rayuela*, Buenos Aires, 1963, p. 139, as is *Le Matin*, p. 466.

[30] In connection with the elusive identity of Fulcanelli, there is a reference to "un tal Berger" (sic) (*A*, 329).

[31] Sabato is probably referring to hypnotically-induced sleep and the *desdoblamiento* possible during it. An incident when this takes place occurs in Valle-Inclán's *Tirano Banderas*. See Emma Speratti-Piñero, *El Ocultismo en Valle-Inclán*, London, 1974, pp. 136-139.

[32] Notices about Rudi Schneider like those included in the *Encyclopedia of the Unexplained*, ed. Richard Cavendish, London, 1974, art: "Rudi Schneider (1908-1957)" and in Nandor Fodor, *An Encyclopedia of Psychic Science*, New Jersey, 1974, art: "Schneider Brothers, Rudi and Willi", for instance, fail to mention Schneider's place of birth. It is, however, given in *Le Matin*, p. 433.

[33] See Konrad Heiden, *Der Fuehrer. Hitler's Rise to Power*, London, 1944, esp p. 198, and *Encyclopedia of the Unexplained*, ed. cit., art: "Atlantis".

[34] It is perhaps worth recalling here the irony of the name chosen by the National Socialist Party. The Second Reich would have been more appropriate. The Third Reich is the Joachite Third Realm, which was to follow the Apocalyptic holocaust of the Second. See Ruth Kestemberg-Gladstein, "The Third Reich", *Journal of the Warburg Institute*, XVIII, 1955, 245-295.

[35] Pauwels' and Bergier's sources are not always reliable, and they are often speculative and inaccurate. One of their main sources for the theory that Hitler was a medium comes from Rauschning, a reliable source on this occasion, according to Alan Bullock, *Hitler. A Study in Tyranny*, Harmondsworth (Pelican Books), 1962, p. 375. It is the French translation of Rauschning's book that suits their case better than the English original. Rauschning talks of Hitler's undistinguished personality coupled with the sudden changes which completely transformed it. He adds: "there is an instructive parallel—mediums". Hermann Rauschning, *Hitler Speaks*, London, December 1939, p. 252. But the French text quoted in *Le Matin* reads: "on est obligé de penser aux médiums" (*Le Matin*, p. 434).

[36] "L'occultisme enseigne qu'après s'être concilié des forces cachées par un pacte, les membres du groupe ne peuvent évoquer ces forces que par l'intermédiaire d'un magicien, lequel ne saurait agir sans un médium" (*Le Matin*, p. 434).

[37] *A*, 80 and *Le Matin*, p. 441.

[38] "La façon dont le mercure peut être ainsi imprégné a été gardé secrète par ceux qui savaient et constitue probablement une porte vers quelque chose de plus noble (que la fabrication de l'or) qui ne peut être communiqué sans que le monde coure à un immense danger, *si les écrits d'Hermès disent vrai*." (My italics). Note that Sabato has removed italicised phrase. Pauwels and Bergier give their source as *Newton Tercentenary Celebrations*, Cambridge, 1947. Their quotation, accurate and complete (*Le Matin*, p. 149), comes from "Newton" by Prof. E. N. da C. Andrade, F.R.S. (U.K.), p. 19, who also implies that Newton might have known about nuclear fission. The same text is in Prof. Andrade's book, *Sir Isaac Newton*, London, 1961, pp. 117-8.

[39] Quoted by Puech, op. cit., p. 201.

[40] Correa, op. cit., p. 21.

[41] There is an interesting parallel (others will be discussed presently) between this episode and the painter Victor Brauner's foreknowledge of the loss of one of his eyes. In an attempt to explain this notorious event, Dr Pierre Mabille says the following: "On est en droit de chercher dans le passé de Brauner si un choc psychique grave n'est pas venu à un moment donné charger l'œil d'un complexe particulier. On apprend en effet que, pendant son adolescence en Roumanie, notre ami a été ému par le récit d'un scandale mondain: un jeune homme de la haute société avait écrasé les deux yeux d'une femme riche et âgée qui l'entretenait et qui au moment de l'attentat se livrait à des embrassements particuliers". (Pierre Mabille, "L'œuil du peintre", *Minotaure*, Vol. 12/13 May 1939, 54). Mabille also reproduces the painting and drawings that linked eyes and sex for Brauner, as they do for Sabato. It is impossible to say whether there is more than a parallel between Mabille's explanation—the *choc* to the adolescent Brauner—and Sabato's school episode. Sabato may well have been persuaded by Mabille and have decided to introduce a similar incident in *Abaddón*, for it does not seem to be based on fact (?) (Neyra, op. cit., p. 14). Juan Larrea explains the "caso Brauner" in different terms; see Juan Larrea, *Del Surrealismo a Machupicchu*, Mexico City, 1967. Most of Mabille's illustrations are also found in Larrea.

[42] I shall go on using the Spanish, not only because Sabato uses it, but because it is simpler than "out-of-the-body experiences", used by C. D. Broad, *Lectures on Psychical Research*, London, 1962, who treats the subject with the utmost respect. See Nandor Fodor, op. cit., art: "Double" where various terms and theories are discussed.

[43] See Lilia Dapaz Strout, *"Sobre héroes y tumbas*: misterio ritual y purificación de la carne", *Novelistas hispanoamericanos de hoy*. Ed. Juan Loveluck, Madrid, 1976, pp. 197-235; and *"Sobre héroes y tumbas:* mito, realidad y superrealidad", *Homenaje a Ernesto Sábato*, Ed. Helmy F. Giacoman, New York, 1973, pp. 361-373. "Duality" and "doubles" were, of course, a commonplace during an earlier "boom" of the occult at the turn of the century. See Pamela Bacarisse, *"A Confissão de Lúcio*: Decadentism *après la lettre"*, *Forum* X, 1974, 156-174 and J. Ann Duncan, *Les Romans de Paul Adam*, Berne, 1977.

[44] "Matilde de quien estaba practicamente separado, agotada la paciencia, regresó a Buenos Aires". María Angélica Correa, op. cit., pp. 61-2.

[45] Page 157 of Paul Foote's translation, Harmondsworth, 1966.

[46] Brauner's 1927 drawing of the lower half of the body of a woman with such a sex, reproduced by Mabille and Larrea (see above, note 41) was known to Sabato, as he admits in the novel: "cuadros [de Brauner] en los cuales el ojo es sustituido por un sexo femenino" [sic] (*A*, 341). He must surely mean the reverse: "el sexo sustituido por un ojo". Several of Brauner's works were recently seen in the Hayward Gallery in London, but not this drawing. See *Dada and Surrealism Reviewed*. Catalogue of the Exhibition by Dawn Adas: Arts Council of Great Britain, 1978.

[47] Quoted by Marina Warner, *Alone of All her Sex. The Myth and Cult of the Virgin Mary*, London, 1976, p. 58.

[48] Charles-Henri Puech, "Phénoménologie de la gnose", op. cit., p. 194.

[49] *Le Mystère des cathédrales*, p. 90.

[50] Jonas, op. cit., p. 45. C.-H. Puech, op. cit., p. xix.

[51] "Les Nicholaïtes et les Gnostiques d'Épiphane paraissent s'être livrés aux pires excès. Pour justifier les mœurs impures que l'on pratiquait, les uns soutenaient que *le vrai gnostique doit tout éprouver;* c'est ainsi qu'il se montre supérieur à la tentation. D'autres, adoptant la doctrine de Marcion, sous prétexte que le créateur est l'ennemi, et que l'on doit détruire son oeuvre, prenaient le contre-pied de la nature". Eugène de Faye, *Gnostiques et Gnosticisme. Étude critique des documents du Gnosticisme Chrétien aux IIème et IIIème siècles*, Paris, 1913, p. 458.

[52] *SHT*, 410-429.

[53] Ibn Arabi, to whose "night journey" Sabato makes passing reference (*A*, 295), befriended Fatima of Córdoba who, as Henry Corbin tells us, "despite her advanced age [. . .] possessed such beauty and grace that she might have passed for a girl of fourteen". Henry Corbin, *Creative Imagination in the Sufism of Ibn Arabi*, London, 1969, p. 40.

[54] I am indebted to Professor D. J. Gifford for my invaluable map of Buenos Aires.

[55] Ángela Dellepiane does not share, either, the doubts some critics have expressed about the identity of the woman Fernando is to meet in the crypt of the Belgrano Church. I do not think there can be any doubt that "sé que ella me estará esperando" refers to Alejandra. See Ángela Dellepiane, *Sábato, un análisis de su obra*, Buenos Aires, 1970, p. 195. This is a virtual reprint of her earlier book, quoted above, note 17.

[56] See above, p. 197.

[57] Nacho treats literary characters as real people. He appends to a photograph of Flaubert the caption: "Pero ella se suicidó, asqueroso" (*A*, 68).

[58] "On appelle ou peut appeler "gnosticisme"—et aussi "gnose"—toute doctrine ou toute attitude religieuse fondée sur la théorie ou sur l'expérience de l'obtention du salut par la Connaissance." Charles-Henri Puech, "Phénoménologie de la Gnose", op. cit., p. 185. "La gnose est une expérience ou se réfère à une expérience intérieure inamissible, par laquelle, au cours d'une illumination qui est régénération et divination, l'homme se ressaisit dans sa vérité, se ressouvient et reprend conscience de soi, c'est-à-dire, du même coup, de sa nature et de son origine authentiques." Ibid., p. 190.

[59] Op. cit., p. 66.

[60] Op. cit., p. 174.

[61] It was published separately in *DAVAR* (1964), No. 160, pp. 84-98, and, not having been used in *SHT*, is now incorporated here, somewhat anticlimactically. It re-echoes, in less emphatic terms, the cycle of life implied in Lavalle's death: "(¿para convertirse en árbol, en planta, en perfume?)" *SHT*, 464, and is largely autobiographical (Neyra, op. cit., p. 16).

[62] Op. cit., p. xix.